DAVID'S COPY

MECHANICS' INSTITUTE LIBRARY
57 Post Street
San Francisco, CA 94104
(415) 393-0101

D0311543

MECHANICS-
MERCANTILE
LIBRARY.

Arthur F. Mathews '06

DAVID'S COPY

THE SELECTED POEMS OF
DAVID MELTZER

Introduction by Jerome Rothenberg

Edited with a Foreword by Michael Rothenberg

MECHANICS' INSTITUTE LIBRARY
57 Post Street
San Francisco, CA 94104
(415) 393-0101

Penguin Poets

PENGUIN BOOKS
Published by the Penguin Group
Penguin Group (USA) Inc., 375 Hudson Street, New York, New York 10014, U.S.A.
Penguin Group (Canada), 90 Eglinton Avenue East, Suite 700, Toronto, Ontario,
Canada M4P 2Y3 (a division of Pearson Penguin Canada Inc.)
Penguin Books Ltd, 80 Strand, London WC2R 0RL, England
Penguin Ireland, 25 St Stephen's Green, Dublin 2, Ireland (a division of Penguin Books Ltd)
Penguin Group (Australia), 250 Camberwell Road, Camberwell,
Victoria 3124, Australia (a division of Pearson Australia Group Pty Ltd)
Penguin Books India Pvt Ltd, 11 Community Centre, Panchsheel Park,
New Delhi – 110 017, India
Penguin Group (NZ), cnr Airborne and Rosedale Roads, Albany,
Auckland 1310, New Zealand (a division of Pearson New Zealand Ltd)
Penguin Books (South Africa) (Pty) Ltd, 24 Sturdee Avenue,
Rosebank, Johannesburg 2196, South Africa

Penguin Books Ltd, Registered Offices:
80 Strand, London WC2R 0RL, England

First published in Penguing Books 2005

10 9 8 7 6 5 4 3 2 1

Copyright © David Meltzer, 2005
All rights reserved

Grateful acknowledgment is made for permission to reprint the following copyrighted works:
"Millennial" from Arrows: Selected Poetry 1957–1992 by David Meltzer. Copyright © 1994 by
David Meltzer. Selections from No Eyes: Lester Young by David Meltzer. Copyright © 2000
by David Meltzer. Reprinted by permission of Black Sparrow Books, an imprint of David R.
Godine, Publisher, Boston. Selections from Beat Thing by David Meltzer. Reprinted by per-
mission of La Alameda Press, Albuquerque, New Mexico.

Other selections in this book first appeared in the author's earlier publications; see the bibli-
ography on pages 259–261 for a complete listing.

LIBRARY OF CONGRESS CATALOGING IN PUBLICATION DATA
Meltzer, David.
    David's copy : the selected poems of David Meltzer / introduction by Jerome Rothen-
berg; edited with a foreword by Michael Rothenberg.
      p. cm.
    Includes bibliographical references.
    ISBN 0-14-303618-1
    I. Rothenberg, Michael. II. Title.
PS3563.E45A6 2005
811'.54—dc22   2005043374

Printed in the United States of America
Set in Galliard with Akzidenz Grotesk
Designed by Sabrina Bowers

Except in the United States of America, this book is sold subject to the condition
that it shall not, by way of trade or otherwise, be lent, resold, hired out, or otherwise
circulated without the publisher's prior consent in any form of binding or cover
other than that in which it is published and without a similar condition
including this condition being imposed on the subsequent purchaser.

The scanning, uploading and distribution of this book via the Internet
or via any other means without the permission of the publisher is illegal and
punishable by law. Please purchase only authorized electronic editions,
and do not participate in or encourage electronic piracy of copyrighted
materials. Your support of the author's rights is appreciated.

811
ms29d

To the fallen
and the arising

Acknowledgments

Impossible to scroll up or down all those who supported and published my work through the decades, but I'll try (and regret any absences).

First of all, before anybody else, Michael Rothenberg and Terri Carrion and Jerome Rothenberg.

Then roll scroll: Donald and Alice Schenker, Frederick Roscoe, Peter LeBlanc, Wallace Berman, Dave Haselwood, Robert Alexander, John Martin, Kenneth Rexroth, Melissa Meytinger, Robert Durand, Jack Shoemaker, Graham Mackintosh, Robert and Dorothy Hawley, James Brook, Christopher Winks, Diane DiPrima, Leroi Jones, Jack Hirschman, Asa Benveniste, Maxine Chernoff, Larry Fagin, Duncan McNaughton, William Margolis, Franco Minganti, John McBride, Michael McClure, Kristine McKenna, Michael Perkins, Howard Schwartz, Michael Castro, John Brandi, Giovanni Singleton, James R. Willems, Karl Young, Jessica Tyler York, Gloria Frym, Aya Rose Tarlow, Victoria Shoemaker, Sylvester Pollet, J. B. Bryan, Paul Slovak, Nancy Peters, Lawrence Ferlinghetti, Thomas Rain Crowe, George Herms, Bob Kaufman, Marina Lazarra, Liz Pintchuck, Matthew Milos, Donald M. Allen, Samuel and Anne Charters, Clark Coolidge, Steve Dickison, Michael Gizzi, Marsha Getzler, Peter Howard, Alan Kaufman, Basil and Martha King, Mary Kerr, Nathaniel Mackey, Frank Rios, Lawrence Welsh, Micah Ballard and Sunnylyn Thibedaux, Ryan Newton, Tisa Walden, Gg Re, Robert Briggs, Kevin Ring . . . blur into fade-out.

Contents

Foreword

Editing *David's Copy* was more than arranging a body of work in an attempt to give a sense of an entire career; it was a collaboration, a transcontinental improvisation, sending boxes of poems back and forth between California and Miami, deciding which poems stay and which poems go, with some revision, and questions. As it unfolded, Meltzer's vision was a revelation, an opportunity to witness the poet seeking god in a letter.

When I read David's poetry, read his words, I think of alchemical conjuring, zen, beat, jazz rhythms, prayer, the everyday in a moment-flash, historical overviews, urban and domestic reflections. Meltzer's work is sly and sardonic, twisted and awkward, nondoctrinaire, agit-smut in the face of love and desire, a commentary of "the real" that goes through a surreal/abstract filter, or *is* surreal. The lyric, the "spoken word," the rant, the list, the journal, and the narrative, he does it all, takes on various personae—alter egos, female, male, and a dog.

David's Copy is a re-visioning of a poetic oeuvre, a selected moment in time, a songster's ecstatic epic-journey, the journey of a "savage word slinger" rummaging relentlessly through iconic shards and celluloid of culture, pop, and hermetic images and language, tempered with humor and love.

Michael Rothenberg
Miami
September 2004

Introduction

I first became aware of David Meltzer—as many of us did—with the publication in 1960 of Donald Allen's anthology, *The New American Poetry,* which celebrated the emergence over the previous decade of a new & radical generation of American poets. Those included ranged in age from Charles Olson, already fifty, to David Meltzer, then in his early twenties. Meltzer's four poems were all short, filling up most of three pages, & displayed a sure-footed use of the kind of demotic language & pop referentiality that was cooking up in poetry as much as it was in painting. His lead-off poem mixed traditional Japanese references with more contemporary ones to Kirin Beer & Havatampa cigars, but there was otherwise no indication of a wider or deeper field of reference—as in the work, say, of older contemporaries such as Olson & Robert Duncan, or of Ezra Pound or William Carlos Williams or Louis Zukofsky before them. Like many of our generation his aim was not to appear too literary; as in the conclusion of his biographical note: "I have decided to work my way thru poetry & find my voice & the stance I must take in order to continue my journey. Poetry is NOT my life. It is an essential PART of my life."

It took another decade of journeying for Meltzer to emerge as a poet with a "special view" & with a hoard of sources & resources that he would mine tenaciously & transform into unique poetic configurations. For me the sense of him had changed & deepened some years before I got to know him as a friend & fellow traveler. The realization—as happens with poets—came to me through the books that he was writing & publishing & that I was getting to read—on the run, so to speak, like so many others. In *The Dark Continent,* a gathering of poems from 1967, I found him moving in a direction that few had moved in—or that few had moved in as he did. The "transformation," as I thought of it, appeared about a quarter of the way into the book—a subset of poems called *The Golem Wheel,* in which the idiom & setting remained beautifully vernacular but the frame of reference opened, authoritatively I thought, into new or untried worlds.

The most striking of those worlds was that of Jewish lore & mysticism, starting with the Prague-based legend of Rabbi Judah Loew & his Frankensteinian creation (the "golem" as such), incorporating a panoply of specific Hebrew words & names along with kabbalistic & talmudic references & their counterparts in a variety of popular contexts

(Frankenstein, the Mummy, Harry Bauer in the 1930s *Golem* movie, language here & there from comic strips, etc.). It was clear too that the judaizing here—to call it that—was something that went well beyond any kind of ethnic nostalgia, that he was in fact tapping into an ancient & sometimes occulted stream of poetry, while moving backward & forward between "then" & "now." In an accompanying subset, *Chthonic Fragments,* a part of it presented in the present volume, he expanded his view into gnostic, apocryphal Christian, & pagan areas that left their mark, as a kind of catalyst, even when he swung back to the mundane 1960s world: the "dark continent" of wars & riots, the funky sounds of blues & rock & roll, the domestic pull of family & home.

I mention this as a recollection of my own very personal coming to Meltzer & to the recognition that he was, like any major artist, building a special world: a meltzer-universe in this case that spoke to some of us in terms of our own works & aspirations. ("The Jew in me is the ghost of me," began one stanza in *The Golem Wheel,* & I was smitten.) His pursuit of origins of all sorts was otherwise relentless—not only in his poems but with a magazine & a press that also took as their point of departure or entry the hidden worlds of Jewish kabbalists & mystics. The magazine was called *Tree* (*etz hayyim,* the tree of life, in Hebrew) & was connected as well to a series of anthologies of his devising (*Birth; Death; The Secret Garden: An Anthology of the Kabbalah*), alongside chronicles of jazz writing & jazz reading & of poetry—Beat & other—that had emerged or was emerging from the place in California where he lived & worked.

What was extraordinary here was the lighthearted seriousness of the project—a freewheeling scholarship in the service of poetry—& his ability to cast an esoteric content in a nonacademic format & language. In this he shared ideas & influences with a range of contemporary artists & poets—notably the great West Coast collagist Wallace Berman, whose appropriations of the Hebrew alphabet as magic signs & symbols led directly to what Meltzer, borrowing a phrase from Allen Ginsberg's *Howl,* called Bop Kabbalah. It was also in that California ambience that he made contact with older poets like Robert Duncan, Jack Spicer, & Kenneth Rexroth, & with younger ones like Jack Hirschman, engaged like him in the search for old & new beginnings. In circumstances where everything suddenly seemed possible, he joined with his wife Tina (as singer) & with fellow poet Clark Coolidge (as drummer) to form a rock performance group called Serpent Power—the name itself an echo of ancient yogic & tantric practice.

The totality of Meltzer's work will wait for another occasion—a Meltzer Reader perhaps or a Collected Meltzer—in which all of it can be mirrored. For now—& not for the first time—he has condensed his nearly half century of poetry into the pages of this book. As such it is a reflection of where he has worked & lived, often with great intensity—first in polyglot New York (Brooklyn to be exact) & later (most of his life in fact) in California. He has never been a great traveler, in the literal sense, but his mind has traveled, metaphorically, into multiple worlds. In the process he has drawn from a multiplicity of times & places & set them against his own immediate experience. His attitude is that of a born collagist, a poet with a taste for "pilfering," he tell us, or paraphrasing Robert Duncan: "Poets are like magpies: they grab at anything bright and they take it back to their nest, and they'll use it sooner or later." And he adds, speaking for himself: "I use everything, everything that shone for me."

The range of the work itself follows from another dictum: "Poems come from everywhere." As such, the focus moves from the quotidian, the everyday, to the historical &, where it fits, the transcendental. The mundane stands out, for example, in a poem like "It's Simple," though not without its underlying "mystery." Thus, in its opening stanza (the whole poem elsewhere in this book):

It's simple.
One morning
Wake up ready
For new work.
Pet the dog,
Dog's not there.
Rise & shine
Sun's not there.
Take a deep breath.
No air.

If the presentation here gives the appearance of simplicity—something like what Meltzer calls "the casual poem"—we can also remember his warning that "art clarifies, it doesn't simplify," that his intent as a poet

is, further, "to write of mysteries in language as translucent and invit-
ing as a mirror."

Mystery or "the potential of mystery" is a term that turns up often in
Meltzer's *poetics*—his talking about the poetry he & others make. It is
no less so where the poem is family chronicle than where it draws on
ancient myth or lore: the fearful presence in *The Golem Wheel:*

> . . . returning home to a hovel
> to find table & a chair
> wrecked by Golem's fist

or the celebration & lamenting of the parents in "The Eyes, the
Blood":

> My father was a clown,
> my mother a harpist.

There is a twofold process in much of what he does here: a *demytholo-
gizing* & a *remythologizing,* to use his words for it. In this sense what is
imagined or fabulous is brought into the mundane present, while
what is mundane is shown to possess that portion of the marvelous
that many of us have been seeking from Blake's time to our own.[1]

David's Copy is full of such wonders, many of them excerpts from
longer works that show a kind of *epic* disposition—in the sense at least
of the *long poem* as a gathering of fragments/segments/image-&-data-
clusters. Watch him at work, full blast, in the two excerpts from
Chthonic Fragments or in the "Hero" & "Lil" excerpts from what was
originally his long poem *Hero/Lil,* in which he draws the Lil of the
poem (= Lilith, Adam's first wife; later, the mother of demon babes)
into the depths of post-exilic life:

> She-demon deity
> lies on the sofa
> stretching like a cat.

---

[1]Writes Meltzer further, in our talking through of it: "To demythologize means
countering that person or product or event made mythic, somehow emptied of
complexity; to remythologize is to pick up cast-off debris from the assembly line &
rework (like assemblage & collage) into new & more problematic relationships—I do
take the two words as two distinct actions, intrusions, or interventions."

Small hot breasts.
Miles breathes "Blackbird."
She accepts
the hash and grass joint.
Cool fingers
dive under my pants
ka! ka! ka!
Screech of all
Lil's hungry babies
caged-up next door.

Or again:

She wants words only at dawn.
I touch her mouth with language
then afterwards move against her.

In other serial works the touch is lighter, where he observes or play-fully takes the role—totemlike—of magical yet ordinary animal beings: the dog in *Bark, A Polemic,* says:

Bark is what us dogs do here in Dogtown
also shit on sidewalks doormats porches trails
wherever new shoes walk fearless.
Bark is what us dogs do here in Dogtown
it's a dog's life
we can't live without you.
Mirror you we are you.
Beneath your foot or on the garage roof.
You teach us speech bark bark
for biscuits we dance for you.
You push us thru hoops
& see our eyes as your eyes
but you got the guns the gas the poison
all of it.
Bark is what us dogs do here in Dogtown.

Or the Monkey in the singular poem of that name—both pseudo-orthodox ("Bruised before Yahweh") & quasi-stylish ("Suave in my tux").

These are the marks of a poet who has worked over a span of time, to pursue interests near & dear to him. To cite another instance, *music*—the full range of it for Meltzer—comes into a larger portion of the poems, a reflection of his own musical strivings inherited in part from his harpist mother & cellist father, celebrated in the long poem or poem series *Harps,* itself a section from a much longer ongoing work called *Asaph,* one intention of which is to use music, he tells us, "as a form of autobiography." Of such musically engaged works the great example is his recent book-length poem for Lester Young, *No Eyes,* from which he has generously selected for the present volume. Add to that another big work, *Bolero* (also a part of *Asaph*), & short poems or references to Hank Williams (the "lamentation" for him), Billie Holiday ("Darn That Dream"), & Thelonious Monk, among recurrent others. Later too, when he becomes a chronicler (*Beat Thing* the most recent & most telling example), the music of the time, like its poetry & loads of pop debris & rubble, has a place at center.

I would cite *Beat Thing* in particular as both his newest book as of this writing & as something more & special: a harbinger perhaps of things to come. As recollection & politics, it is Meltzer's truly epic poem—an engagement with recent history (the 1950s) & his own participatory & witnessing presence. If the title at first suggests a nostalgic romp through a 1950s-style "Beat scene," it doesn't take long before mid-twentieth-century America's urban pastoralism comes apart in all its phases & merges with the final solutions of death camps & death bombs from the preceding decade. This is collage raised to a higher power—a tough-grained & meticulously detailed poetry—"without check with original energy," as Whitman wrote—& very much what's needed now.

The reader of *David's Copy* will find in the more recent poems that end it a sense of timeliness amid the timelessness that poetry is often said to offer—*Beat Thing* clearly but also *Reds vs Feds, Tech,* or even *Shema 2* with its linking of judaic supplications & koranic language in the wake, I would imagine, of the ongoing Israeli-Palestinian conflict.[2] The political engagement—embedded in the poetry itself—is both real & heedful of

[2]Meltzer further: "*Shema* confronts all wars as Holy & challenges the redemptive possibility of faith in the face of the strip-mining-out of the betrayed core tenets."

his earlier remarks that looked down at the "one-dimensionalizing" of so much political poetry ("a tendency to supply people with conclusions, but you don't give them process") in contrast to which "a certain kind of pornography was what I wanted to do as politics." And that in fact was something that he also did—a genre of novel writing that he called "agit-smut" & described as "a way for me to vent my rage and politicize . . . a way of talking about power."

Elsewhere, in speaking about himself, he tells us that when he was very young, he wanted to write a long poem called *The History of Everything*. It was an ambition shared, maybe unknowingly, with a number of other young poets—the sense of what Clayton Eshleman called "a poetry that attempts to become responsible for all the poet knows about himself and his world." Then as now it ran into a contrary directive: to think small or to write in ignorance of what had come before or in deference to critic-masters who were themselves, most often, nonpractitioners & nonseekers. By contrast, as is evident throughout this book, Meltzer allied himself with those poets of his time & place (Beats & San Francisco Renaissance & others) who were both international in their range & the true carriers or creators of traditions new & old.

It was in the course of such experimentation that I met him, & his companionship added immeasurably to my own work as a poet. The body of his work by now is comprehensive, & *David's Copy* offers us a map or template for its comprehensiveness. Since it's David's *selection* as well, it reflects as such the intensity of what another tribal people (or their interpreters) spoke of as "reality at white heat." It's for that reality—both discovered & constructed—that we've been searching, & it's a version of that search & its consequences that *David's Copy* offers to its readers.

Jerome Rothenberg
Encinitas, California
September 2004

DAVID'S COPY

Now for Instance the Idiot

Now for instance the idiot
who watches through the slit eye
and tilted head

a mouth that smiles without a sense of humor
watch him watching you
and know that he sees you

without smiling

. . . from an untitled long poem

Somewhere, waiting to be found; a bar-mitzvah of hopelessness in the Waldorf Cafeteria, hungering for the chance to detonate New York, return the Masses to themselves; hungering, waiting to be found, rejoicing in Joyce because he confused, needing little magazines because they refused, rejecting the scholar because he seemed too safe and all-knowing; he had nothing to tell me, sitting in the Waldorf Cafeteria, wondering where Bohemia was; in some backalley of the Village, waiting to be stumbled into.

Youngest radical to join the back-lines: all waiting for their chance to step out of the line and proclaim an action that never happened; to throw a time-bomb in the marble echo of a bank, or tie T.N.T. to the feet of the Brooklyn Bridge; to topple the statue of George Washington in Wall Street; start a chain-reaction of burning dresses in the Garment Center; to paint Harlem in Jazz; to free the enslaved; to enslave the enslavers; to do anything, but to do something final: act for the turmoil wanting form inside.

Folk-singing prophets in mid-afternoon: sandle-squeekings in Washington Square: the Zionist zombies sipping cafe espresso a long way from Israel, whispering hatred towards orthodox Jewry: Itkin, the impossible, on the steps of the Catholic Church, confused by T. S. Eliot, wishing he was not queer: the lisp and laugh of the fairies, snipping perfume through the urinated streets of Greenwich Village: the nights of the blackened days, benzedrine blues, and flowers early in the morning, walking home and stepping on scattered petals, the pollen within crying its own fertile soil, and waiting to be known.

Uniforms of black; disciples of the castrated ball; we danced in the Waldorf, turned on in the Automat, threw ourselves in front of the A train in order to know motion; we were living visions of weekly suicides, crawling into hangouts with our bandages dripping and our rebellions slipping.

Somewhere, waiting to be found; we fooled the fakirs; we were the kings of the low-world; we were maggots in some foul armpit; there was no loving, only the desire to love, and waiting waiting.

This was just the genesis one, the beginning; we were to be away; discovering Zen, spiritualism, Norman Vincent Peale, the positive, the negative; even then, whisper of Sartre and the Paris Existentialism.

I followed; never found; and no one celebrated my bar-mitzvah in the Waldorf Cafeteria, not even myself, who felt older than timelessness, and sought death; in poetry, in people, in passing through to loveliness.

MECHANICS' INSTITUTE LIBRARY
57 Post Street
San Francisco, CA 94104
(415) 393-0101

Vision

The heart sees
what the mind sees
what the eyes see

differently

2nd Raga: The Woods

It would be morning.
I would awaken, fart & reach
for the joint
cradled in the ashtray,
& turn on. The sun

thru the trees around the house
in the woods of Vashon Island.
Today, I thought (exhaling),

I'll go to the wild patch & pick
a bowlfull of strawberries
for my breakfast.

Brooding in a cage, hooked
above the Menagerie Master's trunk,
a one-legged parrot.
His wings sulk into passive folds.
He lets his tongue widen in
its old chipped beak.

    The lice-fevered bear

        —They put these big leather boots on his
        big stinky feet. His claws are torn out
        —even his dumb teeth are fake!
        DANCE!

Not for a parade, the music

(Down Columbus Avenue (no horses)
simonized Cadillac convertibles carrying paper flowers,
Madonnas of painted plaster, & banners
hanging from the doorhandles.

    The Majorette is 12 & breastless.
  Her kneecaps are greased with dirt & salt.
  The sun illuminates the cheap silks,
  brightly illustrates the gold &
  thin black hairs upon her legs, her arms

Followed by
The North Beach Junior High School R.O.T.C. BRASS
Auxiliary Band:
paratroopers marching thru Roma—
tuba, trumpets, drums. Followed by

The St. Francis Parochial Girls School Percussion Band:
yellow & green silk & braid—
holding up their drums—snare, bass, kettle—
cymbals, triangle, cowbells)

Not for a parade, the music—but
for the dance!
Jubilate Deo omnis terra!

Puncta . puncta . bhm!   bhm!   bhm!

      (Passing the Dunkit Donut Shop.
The tigers in their d.a. hairsets, sit around,
drinking coffee, Cokes, & smoking—looking
out the window to see
the full young girls wiggle by
en route to the Big Boy Supermarket.
The jukebox)

Regular measure—beat of the dance:
estampie, the dance roaring the hall with echo:
fiddles, trumpets, shawm, & viol.
TUMBLERS & ACROBATS! Jugglers
flinging porcelain balls into the apex of
the court's vaulted roof.

      Bean a Deamon! (ROCK
A BABY ROCK A BABY ROCK A BABY BYE!
—Yeah.
Motorcycle—S.F.P.D.—pulls against the curb.
Black suit, white crash helmet, walks into the Dunkit)
Salterello.

Then the peasants are wild with wine,
the need to cool the heat in their groins.
Dancing off to bed or to the secret cove
behind the lemon trees! The bear got sick.

   —Everytime, everytime—give 'em a sip of
   my old man's homebrew & the damn dumb animal
   starts in

Bazza Danza: the peace; formal
glide & flow for whoever's left.
The wagons shake with lovers;
the bushes crackle. Whoever's left,
the Traditionalists, dance the slow dance
correctly. As if the Queen were watching,
looking thru a square lensed telescope—
seawaves & dolphins carved in gold upon it.

Bhm.   Puncta.   BHM!

Look. The caravan breaks camp, begins
moving, passing thru night. (Bird's eye
—the high!) Tinderboxes clank,
clack against the wagons. Soft lights.

From here—a hawk's wingtip
tickling my cheek—it looks like
a reel of astrology's warm stars
going into the forest. The trees
hide everything from the birds.

For Joey Loewinsohn
Age: 4 Months, 9 Days

Angels play accordions too.
Kazoos, ukes, banjos, tubas,
washboards, barrelheads, &
plastic chord organs.

Can't you hear them playing,
loud & cornball,
The Stars & Stripes Forever?

15th Raga / for Bela Lugosi

Sir, when you say
Transylvania or wolfbane
or
I am Count Dracula,
your eyes become wide
&, for the moment, pure
white marble.

It is no wonder (&
not as a putdown either) that
you were so long a junkie.

It's in the smile. The way
you drifted into Victorian bedrooms
holding up your cape like skirts,

then covering her face
as you bent over her to kiss
into her neck & sup.

It is no wonder & it was
in good taste too.

Moon Tunes

1

The black silk cat stretches—
her inner oven roaring softly

& the thinnest black hairs stick
to the weaves of my pants &
the front of my sweater

2

Full moon. Black cat—
she-cat—on my lap,
twisting her belly upwards so
my hands can slide over it,
rubbing the rims of her sex
accidentally

Poem for Tuolumne's First & Last
Artist Investigator of Truth

O earth's women smell as plants
transplanted from dawn's moist soil

& all is dawn now!
The woods around the lumbermill,
the lake sifting thru pebbles on the shore,
yellow grass of the cowpasture,
night's red-eyed dogs sleep in the shade
of tombstones over Pyramid Hill.

Women of the morning (joy)
sweep away dust that night
sprinkled on their porches.
Women born in bed, stretch on them,
their naked flesh soothed by wind
trespassing gently thru
an open window: a goat in the backyard

nibbling at a dried peyote face
secret in the earth

6th Raga / for Bob Alexander

The cigarette gone, you walked
over to the stain where
the sea last hit the shore
&, with your fingers, began
drawing the outline of a woman
into the sand. Her body—
her breasts: a poke
inside each center for
her nipples. Her cunt—
a simple v, & her hair,
a spray of seaweed found nearby,
some twigs.

Jumping back, the sea rushing in,
you yelled out something very loud—
but the ocean was louder.
I didn't hear.
We turned our back on the Pacific,
the mural of your woman,
letting them do battle unseen.
Back up to Ocean Front Avenue.
Charlie was waiting with his camera,
Altoon had arrived with a 6-pack
of good old Lucky Lager Beer.

A Poem for My Wife

I'm in my room writing
speaking in myself
& I hear you
move down the hallway
to water your plants

I write truth on the page
I strike the word over & over
yet I worry you'll pour too much water on the plants
& the water will overflow onto the books
ruining them

If I can't speak out of myself
how can I tell you I don't care about the plants?
how can I tell you I don't care if the books get wet?

We've been together seven years
& only now do I begin
clearing my throat to speak to you.

This Morning

arising to quiet our children,
last night's seed
a trail of light down your thighs.

Self-Portrait

on the window
facing a wall of wood slats

Aww the hell with it!
Recognize the limit

2, 3 feet ahead of me: me
my face on the glass

looking up

The Luna Park Fire

Laughing Lady of rubber bowels
tubes shoved thru turning gears
rocks & laughs on her burning platform

hair a snarl of fire
dress screams with sudden flame
bent over to laugh

the record which is her voice
warps with heat & melts

The Blackest Rose

I'm afraid of the flowers, she said
   they move so quietly.

Vines on the bedtable
   Roses on the dresser
Awaken at night as my breath awaits love
   to come move my room

The flowers turn
   (Breathe as they move)
Towards me, in the dark
   Large shadows

I'm afraid of the breath the flowers have,
   she said

Tonight, new moon, I watch without sleep
   So quietly do they move upon me

Youth Rite Reels

Farewell, my friends, my path inclines to this side of the mountain,
yours to that. For a long time you have appeared further and further
off to me. I see that you will at length disappear altogether.

THOREAU: JOURNALS

1

Home's grip chokes me dizzy
I pound walls to leave this room.

Dresser mirror watches an open window.

Road going into a hill
& beyond it,
the radium of cities.

MECHANICS' INSTITUTE LIBRARY
57 Post Street
San Francisco, CA 94104
(415) 393-0101

2

In the bus, Greyhound deluxe,
one bathroom for all, small
lights overhead like flashlights.
I can't read my book. Passing

black forms, small towns, city neon.
Passing around a cheap fifth of vodka
Discharged today, two soldiers try
to get us all drunk. In the dark
someone starts to sing O Susannah.

I go to sleep in Ohio,
wake up in Omaha.
There's snow all around us
in piles 10 feet high.

3

Factory smoke & jet trails
mark the blue with ghosts.
Moving towards the city,
the car goes fast.
Its driver beeps the horn twice.
This is the way to drive.

Rock & roll on the radio,
wind thru the window,
cigarette sparks.

Wheels turn, I feel them,
on a bump, springs shake,
leaving the sun behind.

Thick clouds form, black
rims slam against sun shafts,
passing by the Edge Motel
(in construction)

a broken water line
pissing up into the coming storm.

4

I sing to them, the old men,
    their faces worn as mesas,
mouths thin as razor slices
    manage can after can of Pearl Beer.

10 gallons halfmast,
    tiny Roy Roger eyes
gleam in shadow.
    They await my flute solo.

Mud in boot,
    I dance from their bullets.
Shaman, it ain't fair,
    turn me to a jackrabbit.

I cry, the sky
    so beautiful blue
with two torn clouds
    hanging,
ready to fall.

A Rent Tract for Lew Welch

At the first of the month I go to the Rental Agency.

—Listen, I tell her, —I can't pay this month's rent because I quit my job because I have a great work that I'm working on that demands a great deal of all my time. My job was a rock in my heart, a black cloud in my head, & I'm a poet who needs time to be alone, to wander, study, loaf & drink, think, read, love my wife, learn about my kids, & work day & night on my great work. I gave this month's rent to my wife for food, diapers & wine. Won't you just forget about rent until my great work is done?

—Sure, she says, writing out a check for $229 (the exact amount to tide us thru a month)—& come back at the first of next month for your next check & turned back to her ledger.

Tishoh B'Ov, 1952

Marty was the first holy man I knew. He was a pale seventeen-year-old rabbinical student at the Yeshiva University.

It was with Marty that I spent Tishoh B'Ov in 1952. We fasted, went to shul, then walked upon the Rockaway Boardwalk, looked at the sea & watched sea gulls strut & scavenge in the sand.

•

Months later, we strolled thru a State Park. Marty was profoundly silent. I was silent, hoping that a Revelation would come into his sacred skull & I'd be there to hear it & humbly transcribe it for all mankind.

We came to an empty playground & sat upon swings, swaying back & forth, our toes gliding thru fall leaves.

Beyond the trees, a highway. I could hear the sound of trucks & cars passing by. Our silence was so huge, I could hear twigs move, I heard the sound of my blood moving thru my veins.

Marty finally spoke.

—Do you see those cars going down the highway?
   I nodded.
—Do you see those trees?
—Yes.
—Do you know what?
—No, Marty, what? I asked of him, keeper of the Great Secret Key to numbers, letters & God.
   Marty spoke softly.
—Bullshit, he said. —They're all bullshit. The trees, the cars, the leaves, your sneakers. Everything is bullshit.

•

To shut my eyes & awaken
   years later
in a yellow stucco room.

Green leaf shadows,
   currents of air,
move over thin curtains.

Feel a cool breeze
   & look down,
dazzled by new white sheets.

Mahshav, Mitva, Miktav

When have I been before You
    to plant my seed, to
sing my song, give room, allow
    my soul a vowel upon Your tongue?

When mountains called
    I did not go
When the woods asked
    I did not go
When in space without face
    I could not fly
I could not decide nor abide
    in faith, my heart alone
against my solitary mind.
    Fate had me
divided by destiny

Throttled by wind,
    the moon in my head,
I stood still, unbent
until a shadow
asked me to the well.

Then I returned to tribal fires,
    there to imagine peaks & ranges,
invent a forest bound by wind,
    a dark land plowed by lion,
serpent & the bleeding woman
    whose invention I am
& whom now I invent

Who leads me thru meander, thru
    this maze of day into night?
in quest for law & form,
    my heart made whole
an open event,
    subtle & unfolding rose,
infinite river
    mixing milk & blood
to blend all elements into element
    as unto One all hearts return.

Oyez!

Thy seed shall be as the stars of heaven.

ST. CLEMENT OF ROME

In hope I offer a fire-wheel,
    12 stars a-sparkle on the black
waters of the well,
    jasmine & rose leaves
stolen from an albino hare
    & 5 lily petals
pilfered from the dove

      knowing stuff of tribute is only for the hand
O Jesus what to awaken the sleeping heart?
    Off with my robes, roll my rings & coins
down cobble, shave my head, set fire to my flesh:
    a star that instinct follows?

    Light thru wound & wings
break thru my back:
    wings of light, wings of snow
O Christos! your four mirrors

    turn the fox blind,
give sight to the mole,
    my face four times
broken in your light
    O Christ!
I seek sight beyond glass

    & offer a fire-wheel,
12 stars a-sparkle on the water's black
    disc, jasmine, rose leaves
stolen from an albino hare & 5
    lily petals pilfered from the dove.

[December 1965]

The Bath

1

Movie over, we draw a bath & in it
  face each other,
legs around hips in wet embrace.

  Splashing in the jug
I upset, then sink our daughter's fleet of
  plastic boats
docked along the tub's rim.

2

Arise with dream speed from the steam.
  Sea beasts
shimmer in fogged mirror. Ah

the dance is the only dance,
a race to cold sheets thru chill hallway.

New Year's Poem: 1967

Why it's my old friend the piper
back from last year's dying, blind
in one eye, one lung lost
hard of hearing, toothless, drinking
blackberry wine from a paperbag

leans on a car to watch the people go by.

from: The Clown (1959) for Wallace Berman

1 / The Unknown, the Classical
Jugglers in Xanadu,
acrobats in Crete.
The essential is always balance.
Swing forward on springed feet,
hands up, spin & reach,
cartwheel, bounce on earth
& roll into a new dance.

Re-mime the beginning
of Time & Dream, insane,
grace. Dazzle the demons
who watch your fall.

Ravens crying: Ave! Ave!
striking him & eaglets
bit & stripped him of his ribbons.
Ave! Ave!

Maccus, Pappus, Cicirrus.
Faces painted on faces,
blossoms on humpback cranky forms.
What we will be:
warty gourd nose bent down
to punch a hole in the chin,
leering toothless mouth
& a patch of flaming hair
sprouts atop the white face.

●

The roots which hold a poem to earth
reach to suck out the wordless instant.
Send out the clowns.
Box & bash each other.
Struck sideways by the goat-bladder.
Goosed by the staff.

He-who-got-slapped first wore the centunclus,
rags & patches for a bull's-eye.
Harlequin's eye-blinking diamonds.
Christ's cross. Diversion is speed.

●

On flag shanked horses
minstrel, drug peddler
wander to stopped wagons
offering amusement.

Medicine show showers handbills
like dove feathers on mud roads
leading to the Church.

Beneath stained-glass, stone demons,
Christ arose thru a trapdoor,
sulphury smoke belched from Nebuchadnezzar's
red-hot furnace scorching papier-mâché Hell.

Machines unwind flying angels,
thunder, wind & Dossenus flees
from God's butt-clubbing love.

Lamentation
for Zap the Zen Monk

Cold grove to grow pot in.
Wet dew sops thru
sleepingbag.
The hibachi's all rusty,
crudded with dove shit,
dung of cranes.

Wind
topples down bamboo tent
& tender flesh bruises.
Only the mind hardens like ice
to crack & melt into a stream

which perhaps
touches roots (like nerve-ends)
closest to this dream of earth.

Lamentation
for Céline

Dead the day Hemingway blew his brains out in Ketchum

Céline died of contagious poison
crawled on hands & knees to our plate
& puked it all out

like Artaud, Rimbaud
he chucked up his gripes
& barfed back at the dogs

Mean Frog doc loved kids
had none, had icey blue eyes
WW I shrapnel in his brain
an electric sander hits a knothole every second

Disorder prophet
healer, wife-beater
one with people who talk to themselves
argue with history's phantoms
confer with shadowy bomb-throwers in burgundy silk suits
framed in cinema alleyways
offering up gold for a bridge or a boat
or Paradise to slay the King murder the Leader

Upstairs, a radio's too loud
a man pounds his head against plaster
a sniper loads up
another man bangs his wife's head open with an iron fryingpan
rushes her howling to the doctor's pigpen salon
& Louis-Ferdinand swabs out the muck
sews her up & out she goes, she & the old man
hold to earth, stumble into Atlantis
knock off a half-pint of Absinthe

Céline was one with men
whose hair grows out of the heart
into the head & onto the chin
Rumplestiltsken wolf-man

Like them he saw thru the world like a worm thru a tomato

Died the day Hemingway blew his brains out in a hunting lodge
in Ketchum, watching a mountain range disappear

Lamentation
for Jack Spicer

Sir, I'm out of touch with stars.
The bar's closed. We go
stumbling down Grant to Columbus
to the Park to somebody's parked car.
Somebody says, Let's all go to Ebbe's.
Says Ebbe, Sure, why not, let's all go.
We're gone in the car, piled in the back
seat, breathing wine on the windowpanes.
This, seven years ago. Tonight

It is pain to realize you're dead,
your last book on the shelf,
your last words to a nation
not indivisible but invisible;
a nation that will never will its mystery to poets
who even in Greece weren't poet enough to handle man
nor touch the dark forms. Gone.
Maybe that night it was Marco
who fell back upon a park bush.

We left him there to sleep.

The Jew in me is the ghost of me
hiding under a stairway

or returning home to a hovel
to find table & a chair
wrecked by Golem's fist

bed broken, my black rags
hanging from his teeth.

Chthonic Fragments: 1

May Day, 1966: Sunday

For George Herms

. . . For the Lord Himself, being asked by a certain person when His
Kingdom would come, said, When the two shall be one, and the outside
as the inside, and the male with the female, neither male nor female.

FROM: *THE SO-CALLED 2D EPISTLE*
OF ST. CLEMENT TO THE CORINTHIANS

•

Bitch mutt cat in heat
screams in the backyard
bush jungle cherrytree
white petals rug the hunt

courted by king cock tom
cat scarred with chipped ear
combat raging burning babes
howl & croon combustive rites
stalk dance & then

impaled bloom to stalk in fire
absolute light corona halo

bitch cat mutt in heat released
zips around the corner
gone

•

Dressed my daughters three in herbs
leaves cut from early morning earth
for a walk downhill & into town

                blessed by King May
drapes garlands of new buds about them
& the girls unused to ceremony
the brass band, look down,
toe cherry petal snow on the lawn

the youngest sights a squirrel
whose tail turns into a bush
the bush perfect with roses

                    •

Ah the dance, the dancers, dancing
girls hold to ribbons
wrapped around the god's
giant erection

skip to & from his oak
hard entry thru sacral membrane

Celebrate, unravel the earth

The bell-ringer swings with delight

Green music
green friction on the grass
crickets, earth grind

Wine song to the first & last star
moonlight all over our flanks

                    •

Birds alert dawn with song

Upon her in grey early light
my arms two white poles
hold me up

still loving her, loving her
all night, we are locked together
welded

rock as one
slowly without mind
as children rock
as plants bend moved by wind

birds overthrow night
the black shadow of my face
upon the mirror of her eyes
rolls into her skull &
my lady finally sleeps

Gentle to remove myself
I find my back wet
chilled by the cold sheet I fall upon

●

A radiant dream of
Jack-in-the-Green.
He offers me a posy
of blue & gold flowers.

Then he's gone,
kindling the bush.
Earth turns to night
but I see no dark,
only bramble burning.

Jack-in-the-Green,
dream-chaser,
over the hill & gone.

MECHANICS' INSTITUTE LIBRARY
57 Post Street
San Francisco, CA 94104
(415) 393-0101

Chthonic Fragments: 2

21 June 66: 1st day of Summer

Ready, friend!
Are we not here drinking
The shaman's drink,
The magician's drink!
We mix it with our drunken tears and drink.

PAPAGO SONG, TRANS. BY RUTH UNDERHILL

•

Vine-child born of lightning, horned
          lunatic poet leads a mad caravan

bawds in bullskin vests ride motorcycles
          around a goaty roaring pack of cowboy dancers
danced around by dogs & panthers, toadies all
          hip & hard-jawed, all
waiting for the night's wipe-out hillside frolick

          Bulldoze the shit-kicking berg
          firecracker chatter & ricochet of bullets

          shoot the cud with cowed farmers
          red-necked lily-faces sexless with fear

Chase down a ram
cut off his balls
a gift for the Mayor's wife
—We're here to bring you dreams
& grain undreamt, a land
bound both to plow & cosmos

Snipe down the owl & fry his brains
toss away his opened eyes
that catch & lodge in thorns
to surprise the harvest & warn the crows

          •

—What does it matter?
he says in the bar
while the rest of them burn the town down.

—They are afraid
& that is why they run & dance & destroy.
Every rider chases his ghost.
Invisible winged harpies screech revenge,
reap carnage, clash in the sky.

They are afraid to live,
they are afraid to die,
they are afraid to face their faces,
face their fear.
Goats are smarter.
What does it matter?

•

Rip out a telephone pole to
    ram down the winery door.

Up & down hill
    tumble in laurel
stuff your heart with asphodel.

Lady, I pour wine on your white belly,
    your slippery hips.

Fresh raw wine O lean legs
    mortal. Golden hair,
a mole on your forehead.

Lady my heart is breaking,
    your eyes are grey
my heart is breaking.

O lady my love is endless
your lips are soft & I bruise them with my beard
    O mortal my heart is breaking.

Girl your father flies airplanes
        your mother rocks a chair
your brother stands before a mirror
        combing out his long brown hair
O my love is endless as my time

        your nipple tough with desire
accident will give you babies
        & the babies will give you laughter
O lady O love my eyes are wine
        my tears are vinegar
my heart is breaking
        my love is endless

Hymnus

She flies before me
    my lungs are her
my belly holds her tongue
    I grope with dim forms

She flies behind me
    when I crawl to a cave
& flies within me
    when I bend to pray

She's behind my eyes
    spying thru retinal blossoms
to see you

She sees nothing
    & sometimes speaks thru me

She's my hand upon your throat
    within your womb
she is in my mouth when I sing

Mother of my brain
    holds a burning lotus above her head
& drives the fire thru me

Marked as Cain
    she leads me thru new dark to light
she is my pain as she is my balm
    she surrounds me from within
& holds my dance to her drum
    & time is her grace

Time to wear all faces back to bone
    alone, to return to the mother
charging our seed with cosmos

She leads me where I must meet her
      & plants me in earth so I will grow
& slowly take my stand upon the globe
      & reach my heart, my song, to God

To take the simple step & vanish into air
      into her, into all

Record Player

A record of the times, my times,
a record I can play in other times to remind me of time,
hear my voice moan like Job.
Sob over my lousy lot.
Curse poverty, cry against circumstance,
attempt serenity by burning incense
stolen from Cost Plus & lit beneath a picture of
a Tibetan Buddha floating in the saddle of a black tiger.

I hear a morning raga when I look out the window at the cherrytree &
down at the garden kept by the old Italian couple & over the trees to
the Bay & the steamers & sailboats. A music of railroads & trucks &
birds before the light is settled. I set down events after they happen.

●

Poets were once four-footed reptiles who were the custodians
of truth in Eden.

●

A record of learning, of what is known, words in books,
words in the air like butterflies.
A mourning record.
Me & the rabbis *kvetching* in the cold clash of ancient fears
A record of my fall.
Adam & Eve & the snakey poet.

From Eden Book

O snarled in mid-afternoon
Doom in every word
Squadrons of boos & hornets
Drift in blue cloudless sky
Shift as the warm wind blows

Man & motorbike
Buzz thru the redwood grove
Whining growl in the valley
Louder than the entire
Airborne dragonfly patrol

•

Midpoint now
Heart grows tighter
Nerves bunch up more frequently
Snap like an alligator
At flapping hands
All waving goodbye

The earth is harder to break thru
The music richer
With history geology
The cardiogram sounds
Richter scales
Midpoint body
More cock-crazy than ever

Keep our garden green!

•

My children before TV
more concerned with two
turtles in a white porcelain
bowl, 2 rocks &
a couple raggy flags of lettuce
than a cartoon roughneck
fighting off the Dragon.

Dogs bark in the hills.
Loud gossip. Pride of poets.
Chain-verbs broken apart
into abrupt explosions.
Band-saw gargling scream
like the motorbike
as it cuts down another tree
to make room for a swimmingpool
dug into hillside earth.

Sunlight grows brighter
for want of the forest.
Even Eden was a forest.
We return to daily.

So many ways to refuse
tidal black & white
waves of media smashing
brains down, pulping eyes,
slicing a smoking electric road
right down spine's center.

●

We have a garden in the backyard
as meager as you wish.
A grubby clump of radishes,
some brown-leafed dried-up spinach,

Fordhook lettuce nibbled to the roots,
chives, marjoram, basil, some
dillweed, garlic, sagging
tomato plants Safeway-bought
hang like martyrs on the cross,
powdery carrot-tops hopeless,
under-sun-fed.
We have a garden in the backyard
that teaches us what not to grow.
Without proper sunlight,
without proper light,
there is no growth,
no opening-up of bulbs & seeds.
See. You can dig up your own poems
out of the backyard garden.
Bibles are all over the place

●

Wheel of my way. This afternoon
went back with Jane Ellen Harrison
to ancient Greek religion.
Also consulted with *Books in Print*
for Wilhelm Reich titles.
Also sidetracked by
a scrub bluejay attacking
the feeding platform with
nervous beak, squawks & yodels.
Words of kingship, godhood,
god-need hum along with wood-sounds:
birds & dragonflies, bees &
mosquitoes, —there's a hornet
caught between the windows,
banging against the glass,
buzzing. Jane says,
"The religious impulse is directed,

if I am right, primarily
to one end & one only,
the conservation & promotion of life."

O the words snarled in my head.
Mid-afternoon heat.
God dead along with other words.
I've gone backwards
to words revealing only what is left
of holiness, of ecstasy,
what is left of a moment,
left behind in books
bound to be heavy,
bound to be hard carrying up to
Babel's tower-top
& there to see the great New World
bright & loud like Las Vegas
glaring spectrum rainbow color TV
rock & roll hillbilly screaming
sunrise & sunset twang
non-stop electricity power

      O Jerusalem!
your babes all broken
in terror, yowling, bawling
wailing down below, grabbing
at the sky to
pull up into Heaven O
Jerusalem O Eden!
rivers drying up
birds & fish dying
man's rotting brain calcifying
poison breathes into the air
atomic mutant mammals city-crazed
flame throwers in the night
devour diseased food

white as paper in assembly-line
lunch-counter gobbling-up
liver, kidney, heart instant death

O Heaven O Eden O Jerusalem
this afternoon I read Jane Ellen Harrison
in our Marin tree-house
in a valley serenaded by
birds & bees & motorbikes & band-saws & saw
trees topple & the tractors
rip out more earth
leveling soil for new towers,
new Babel foundations,
radio up full-blast,
stereo glass-breaking shatter
of new noise, new clatter
racket chatter of billions & billions of new human beings
raging & roaring about life on the planet
piled upon piles of arms & legs & tits &
cocks & cunts & mouths & sweat shit & piss
in piles in great Pyramids writhing
O new Egypt! rising up to greet white nuclear sun
blazing burning-out the green,
ray-gun fire of factories vomit death into the sky,
green shoots broken-down by steerage tonnage
human race in Dachau! Jerusalem!
O Heaven O Eden!
we are killing each other at last
we are killing each other again
we are clearing the earth of man
we are saying No as loud as we can
in cars crashing head-on on freeways, skyways
smoking cancer, drinking strokes
raping land, fucking our women with more mewly kids
O Jerusalem O Heaven O Eden
genes popping apart in freak collisions

death-dust sprinkled on all our food
stiff fish float topside on oil-slick seas
the seas retreat into desert
whose sand hardens into highways woven upon each other
& soon piled up like great abstract golems
casting an endless shadow of moon-night
upon the ruined visions of Eden
of Heaven of Jerusalem

•

Oh but that's easy, she says.
He says it too.
It's easy.
Apocalypse is poetry's easiest song.
We're not scared, they sing together,
arms around each other.
We're not scared.
Let it roar.

•

Mid-afternoon white wine revery.
Put the book away with all the other books.
I am surrounded by books.
To my right, books.
Behind me, staring at my neck,
book spines, not all of them read.
To my left, another shelf of books
& a window above them
where I see ivy,
drooping purple fuchsias like
pulp science-fiction plants,
thorny-edged succulents,
red & violet geraniums,
a gnarled modern-art tree trunk,
& a clear cloudless blue sky

rattles as the earth beneath me shakes
in sonic-boom clap of crashing space.
Books jiggle on the shelves.
Flowers tremble in the echo
but hold firm, stand their ground.
Delicacy's secrets are there to see.
A subtle construction holds back Armageddon.

Fred Flintstone does a slow-burn
after being hit on the head
10 times with a thorny club.
Our kids watching it. Sunset.
Treehood & Susy, the two turtles,
get the last heat of sunlight
resting on their rocks
in the white porcelain bowl.

The Argument

It was a tough night.
   Owls & a nightmare hawk
tried breaking thru the bedroom window.
   I heard their wings
slam against the glass,
   the clack of their beaks.

   —But what of it? she asks
out of sleep broken by my poking.
   —What if the bedroom is filled with birds
   real or imagined?
   Go back to sleep.

The Argument: 2

—Oh, you, she hollers,
    with your books on the shelves,
Your poems in folders:
    The words, the words
Like high-tide
    Fill up your room.

    No wonder, no wonder,
I nod out before TV
    Waiting for you
To come to me &
    Sing me a song,
Satisfy my needs,
    Give me a moment out of your time.
No wonder.

The Argument: 3

Tough waitress bangs her hand on the hard wood
    counter, says

        No more of this shit.
        I'm more than human,
        I'm a woman!

Early morning workers watch her
    over thick coffeecup rims &
let her work it out.

Flips the pancake to the ceiling.
    Hope it sticks there forever
along with the bacon-fat stars.

Nature Poem

Absurd.
We talk of progress.

My hair falls out all over the place.
Into a bowl of mushrooms.
What a mess.
How much of it have I swallowed?
Yet I let my hair fall.
Ha.
See how man copes with nature.

My teeth shrink.
Rot into nerve-end threads.
The enamel turns upon itself.
I allow my teeth to disappear.

My face falls into place.
Wrinkles work into folds, crack
& sag over my bent jaw.
I allow my face.

My tongue dries like a prune.
Too much air.
I let my tongue evolve.

Soon I'll be an old man.
Many years ago I was a baby.

Absurd.
We talk of progress.

Notes for a Poem to H. P. Lovecraft

1.
OCCULT NIGHT:
arrange dried sticks of swamp weed
picked exactly at the eclipse fusion

cards with dancers
wear Death's commedia masks

dusts the bowls & globes with phoenix feathers

clears table space for oaken racks
& yes
essential element
THE FULL MOON!
clear & precise.
Each detail
of crater & empty basin
prism-illuminated by
powerful Moon Energy.

She can not deny it.
Look, she says, it lights itself,
& holds the candle
to an ancient star-map.

Scales to oil.
Spirit herb scents.
Sand from Arabia
arranged on the floor
in a circle in a star.

Music by the mammoth Calliope.
Piped thru gilt flutes
trilled by the Axe Man's ghost.
His twisted grin.
Fingertips streak blood lines down the mirror.

Wind whose horrid screeching
reaches inside clammy skin to
pull out nerve-fluid, marrow-power,
essential to great works ahead.

Dead trees crash, scatter dust
against the walls &
glass sprays against face-mask,
punctures mouth-roof.
Bloody tree fountain of man.

The Owls turn into Tigers
& stalk Love's stink
with snarls & teeth
sharpened on iron fenceposts.

2.
ACTORS IN THE PLAY

GRUMBUGH: cursed fiend
finds him a furry being to sup on.
Weeds sprout & shoot
out of his toothy mouth.

EXOPYRE: incest-mad Shape
dancing in Fire, decomposing into
golden ashes. Screaming agony
in order to arise & sing
& burn again! & again! & again!

ARVAT: the Knower
weaves an ice castle
with fingers swift as fishfins.
With magical spear
he diverts snow from the air
& forms it into a Sphere.

Charmed dome-castle
that Arvat, the Knower,
lives in &
breaks bread with the Fox.

KRANTZ: the Golem
made of dung, cragged
by heat—a tragic mesa.
Allowed one song
every hundredth year.
His hand, a single finger of his hand,
takes one century to unbend
& point dead-center
between your eyes!

THE ROSE: grinds green from the bulb
to mark her mouth & draw
green lines around her eyes.
She is the Golem's bride
& doth dance with him
at Aleph fests & Shin parades
& she will bear from his stone seed
gargoyles that perch on
iron-haired trees.

                    [1959]

Sonnet: 1

    O mother
brigged in your cramped ship
    O mother
from your gates, the door of cities
    O mother
your elastic womb is a tunnel to Heaven
    O mother
darkness teaching light
    O mother
uncrate your harp, string it new & test its pedals
    O mother
my mouth reaches for your untried nipples
    O mother
hermit owlfish came out your cave
    O mother
I eat sacred eggs to sing to you
    O mother
in green satin robes
    O mother
in black & white polkadot dress
    O mother
holds me up to the Kodak eye
    O mother
paradox of woman
    O mother
cold Rimbaud blue eyes
    O mother
paradox of woman
    O mother
    Mother!

. . . .

O motherfucker wild animal rage
        pitch-black bitch shadow in the night
digs her fingernails into my chest.
        Three blood lines
scar as a branch, the letter

there until I die.

Songs Earth & Moon
Sing after Supper

Lay hands on love's round ass
lying on the unmade bed.

O the Moon, she sighs
& stretches. Bends her body
into a crescent shape.

We're all moon maidens.
Our wombs hold snowlight
of sperm's radiant fountains.

All Luna's ladies breeze thru Eden
in gowns of starlight, idly chattering
to new blooms bursting,
colors all over the stage.

Love, my lady, then arises
& moves across the bedroom carpet
to clear dishes off the supper table
& put them in the sink.

O sister

O sister
let me tell you of green light.

It surrounds Amanda's hair
when the sun is high & heat waves
move up from wet earth.

O sister
let me tell you of green light.

It turns her face into a magic herb.
Her eyes are jade beams
following my poem.

O sister
let me tell you of green light.

O sister
let me tell you of green light
deep in earth's dark.
Let me tell you of green light
in seeds I place into the soil.

O sister
let me tell you of green light.

It surrounds us day & night
upon our hill. Our hill is green light.

O sister
let me tell you my green vision.
Let me show you my book of leaves.
O sister let me plant you.
Let me love
like green light shining thru plants.

O sister
let me tell you.
Let me tell you.
Let me tell you of green light.

Sonnet: 6

My father becomes my Angel
watching me write
poems about Zohar &
the music of clouds.

I see him
practicing his cello
in the middle of the livingroom.
Sleeves rolled up,
shirt open.
Pulls the bow across the strings
with fury.

I see him angry at me
as I am now angry with my daughters.
Blinding rage.
Woman overwhelms us.

My father is my Angel
watching over me like a piano teacher.

We never understood each other.
That we were different,
that we were the same.
Strangers with the same face.
We never understood we were the same,
we were different.
& now he is my Angel
watching over me
as I write to you
& sing his name
& we are not so different, are we?
You & me & my father.

Flight Poem

8 April 69
United Air Lines

Died to be clouds whose white shapes form
The edges of an Angel's profile

Died to be clouds whose white shapes rise
In monumental columns airplanes fly thru

Died to be clouds whose white shapes are
White words against blue pages of sky

Died to be clouds whose white shapes loom up
Like statues in heroic white forests

The airplane flies thru clouds like a museum-goer
A browser in a bookstore

I see the faces of the dead

I see my Father embrace a cloud
Shaped like a cello

I see my Grandfather Benny
An Old Gold stuck in his lips

I see Uncle Jack
Vomit up black storm clouds

Died to be clouds whose white shapes
Form the edges of an Angel's profile

Luna Tunes: Poems for My Daughters
Jenny, Maggie, & Amanda Rose

1.
Now Luna breaks thru the pages
& winds up propped-up, hooked
to the brass-frame bed's back
grill, swaying back & forth.

She stares at the wall
my shadow moves over.
Back & forth I pace.
Grumbling my poems.
Lion roaring poems.
Boiling water poems.
Dragon exploding poems.
The window rattles.
What does glass know?

My poems are gardens
from my mouth, like
ivy out of Botticelli's
teenage seashell brides.

Luna's an eagle.
Flutters her wings.
Gold coins splash on the rug.

I see her nerve-map light up
like a marvelous pinball machine
celebrating total ultimate
non-tilt victory.

2.
Luna wakes the girls up
with birdsongs learned in
the jungles of Brazil.

What a thrill, they think,
ready to follow her anywhere,
ready to run into the center of the green atom.

I stop them at the door.
Go back kids. It's not real.
It's not really happening.

Macaws, toucans, their flaming feathers
flutter around my head.
A silver-scalloped python
coils around my belly.

I stop them at the door.
Go back kids. It's not real.
It's not really happening.

3.
Luna's a dodo
laying velvety cellophane eggs
whose insides shimmer
with green & purple plants
picked off the hill
beyond the place where
all the poison oak grows.

Luna's dodo song is:
Eeep, eeep, eeep.
But then you knew that all along.

The moon's a neighborhood, a block
        in the mind. The time
when a poet lives at night
        inside a saloon &

lunatic ladies test his power
        over trees & animals,
drag him thru Hell,
        drain him of fire

so he may bravely announce his victory
        thru one of her soft
            white throats.

It's Simple

It's simple.
One morning
Wake up ready
For new work.
Pet the dog,
Dog's not there.
Rise & shine
Sun's not there.
Take a deep breath.
No air.
Look for the sun.
No sun.

It's simple.
Wake up one morning
Ready for new work
& the animals are on strike
With the air, the sea, the
Earth quits us.
Casts us off
Like a sickness in her fiery core.

Letters & Numbers

1

In my 32nd year
counting numbers watching
22 letters dance on a wall chart.
Energy goes to & out of 10
ineffable sefira.
Electric radiant systems
I walk thru,
carry beneath my skin,
sing Paradise *Pardes*
walk down the path to help my wife
(in green & gold light) carry
groceries back to our tree house
up 181 steps carved into earth

2

22 ways to speak,
tell you
God crowns spine's tree,
unwinds vertebral knots.
Light spreads thru flesh I
carry to our bed,
your loins spread
to accept the alphabet
I stutter into your womb

3

22 seeds take hold in your dark earth.
Shake apart into life.
22 seeds take hold, arise.
Life-fire rising up in bright loops
surrounds 6 points
unfolds into thousand petal'd celebration

4

Resting after love
beneath night's bridal ark
cobalt-blue lines outline your body
for the moment
600 thousand new sperm beings
float in the womb's sea

bright starlight
lights up the room

5

22 ways to pulverize the tongue
hack the serpent into 22
new snakes all with my face
the face of my children
busy with tongues that delight in song
argument questions
day & night
no stone unturned
no star unmarked
no lifeline left in exile
all in all
22 ways

6

More than mere
utterance of 32 ways.
It must also be
22 seeds to germinate 22 new
Edens, Edom. Green
circles man returns to
as to the sea to re-
learn source.

7

Tracking down 32 lights
O eternal pinball metaphor
Electric-eyed whore
how we serve you
your round lights
service all your
magic numbers!

8

32 light beams break into rays on the page I
spread black ink over.
Designs, faces, secret code,
imagined Chinese, Hebrew,
Egypt glyphs, Nasorean,
Angel alphabets,
digests of all there is to know
reduced to letters to words.
All there is to know is all that I know.
When there is more
you shall have it.

9

This is the news brought back.
No mystery but in silence of numbers & letters.
I tell my bride
there is no mystery but the moment,
penetration,
when emanations merge & bind together.
Sun halves flaming,
stars inside-out,
the hills tremble
& the green glory of woods
turns desert.
No mystery but in the silence of
numbers & letters waiting our touch.

Infinite breath between each letter
sucked into the heart, each number,
each blacked-out star.

    10
32 sequences
consequences
sing for you
to you
from toe to lotus.
Nerve-tree responsa.

                    [1969]

One

ONE
is what I am
always when I think about
what I am.

One.
Once & for all.
One.

One is also how I know
there are other ones too.
They always guide me
back & forth to one.
Once & for all.

TWO
is what I am
when I am
one with another one

like you & me in
the act of love.
Despite all the poems
we are one
we are two.

Two. Together
always one at a time.
Was it twice
we made love to each other
the other night?

Two is how we
understand one.

[1969]

Vashon Island Light

19
on a 3-day fast
dehydrated.

North wall dissolves into a gold hole,
flaming edges open out into a silver forest.
White-light treetops.
Platinum leaves shake off webs of mercury.
House-big snowflakes
wheel over moss-green mountaintops.
Sparkling rods grow in & out of buffed
aluminum planetoids, spheres
extend into infinity.

Inner angel says, "Go thru,
go thru the wall,
thru light's burning ring,
go to the other side,"
over & over as night falls.

[1956]

from: The Hollywood Poems

1
         De Chirico without Cheracol
saw space where its dead echo opened up
a plain unbroken by the dancers.
Instead
a relic supermarket nobody shops at.
Plaster-of-Paris bust of Augustus
Claude Rains Caesar face-down beneath
a Keinholz table
whose top is blue with Shirley Temple's saucers,
pitchers. Mickey Mouse
wind-up dolls in rows like Detroit.
All tilt out of the running without electricity.
Veils of history,
garments worn in movies, hung on
steel racks at Costume R.K.O.
R. Karo would've used the tower's light.
He'd wear it as a cap to re-route lost energy.

         A Yogi sits in space
above a white line dividing right from left
across a boulevard
named for a fly.
La Cienega.
Designed by De Chirico.
High-noon sun shines on the Yogi
3 inches off the road watching Eckhardt's DNA
bubble & re-fuse in the lights of the Milky Way.

         The Pacific
starts & ends in electricity.
Neon feeds the Fun House signs,
klieglights shine on night games,
juice for TV, radio.
Power millenniums come & go & die in the can
as Happy Ending rainbows fan auras over styrofoam palm trees
surround Studio City.

2

L'Age d'Or in a sportscar.
Wirewheels zoom thru funeral hills.
Radials screech thru Venice oil fields.
Iron dinosaur skeletons bite into bruised clouds.

Speed thru it.
98 mph.
Mission-Orange late noon race thru the Hollywood Hills.
110 mph.
Swerve a curve onto the freeway.
Into it, out of it,
we sit in a fireman-red Porsche Speedster.
Top's down.
Cut thru nomad towns.
Orchards, backyards, fields.
The driver is a moviestar.
We talk of Brahms & Mahler & Webern & Berg
& shit
of farmland ferment
stinks thru electric wire fences.
113 mph.
Pass by code-puffing diesel trucks.
Signs pass by,
lead you to Reno, Tahoe, Vegas.
Pedometer, speedometer, click new numbers every second.
120 mph.
Pass a ranch-style saloon
planted in a grove of gas pumps.
124 mph.
Pass into dusk into night.
Smells like a whorehouse.
Night-blooming jasmine crushed.
Crash thru it.
Pass thru everything.
Hit a bump in the road
which is a rabbit.

The Fire

"A funeral will be held for them.
We will form a procession
And I will tear my coat
And we will bury them
Just as in a funeral for a human,"
says Rabbi Zadle Leshinsky after the fire.
The books burnt:
3 sacred scrolls,
a 600-year-old Mishnah,
a Torah annotated by Maimonides,
an early Kabbalist text
"damaged beyond use."
Well-used books on shelfs in shul,
in the Rabbi's study,
piled on each other like lovers,
the pages thumbed to a time-worn tissue
light is filtered thru.

Fire lights nothing.
It is the light below the light longed for.
Fire turns the page to ash.
Ash in turn is turned into soil
to feed the Tree.

All burns down around the fool.
No Jeremiah, no prophet, no one comes
to suck in smoke & fire,
spit out flame webs
shaped into Heavenly rooms
we could spend Eternity
walking in ever-changing splendor.
Door after door to be opened.

Everything burns down.
Fire serpents bark from exploding bowels of
raging demon dogs.
Fire crashes thru walls like fists.
Bores thru books like light beams.
Words radiate, then expire.
Windows melt back to sand.
I sit room-center piloting the angel-ship
bend towards Paradise.
I read:
"The soul unites with the divine soul in a Kiss."
Ceiling folds up, falls on the chair,
cracks open my skull like a walnut.
Vision over, done with.
12 angels band together
& hose the fire off my skull.
Vision speeds from the room with smoke
pulled back into space,
back into worlds behind worlds
within the rings I work my art thru.

[1969]

Tell them I'm struggling to sing with angels
who hint at it in black words printed on old paper gold-edged by time
Tell them I wrestle the mirror every morning
Tell them I sit here invisible in space
nose running, coffee cold & bitter
Tell them I tell them everything
& everything is never enough
Tell them I'm another cross-wired babbling being
songs coming out all ends to meet & flash above the disc above my brain
Tell them I'm a dreamer, newborn shaman
sitting cross-legged in trance-stupor
turning into the magic feather contemplated
Tell them there are moments when clay peels off my bones
& feeds a river passing faces downstream
Tell them I'm davening & voices rise up from within to startle children
Tell them I walk off into the woods to sing
Tell them I sing loudest next to waterfalls
Tell them the books get fewer, words go deeper
some take months to get thru
Tell them there are moments when it's all perfect
above & below, it's perfect
even moments in between where sparks in space
(terrible, beautiful sparks in space)
are merely metaphors for the void between
one pore & another

[1969]

Lamentation for Hank Williams

—If I can't finish writing a song in 10 minutes
then it aint worth the finishing,
                          said Hank to a reporter.
A camera was busy taking pictures for *Life* magazine.

—I'll never get out of this world alive,
                          wrote Hank in a song
published by Acuff-Rose Sales Inc.
sung for millions at The Grand Ole Opry
recorded by MGM Records

flat-picking his D-28
backed-up by the Drifting Cowboys
night after night & during the days
playing at picnics, rallies
supermarket gala openings

—There's no dreams but bad ones,
                          Hank told Audrey
who told her lover who told the doctor
who could not heal him

places no longer places
velocity of faces
& he burned down, died at 29 of an overdose
kindly rocked to sleep in the backseat of his Cadillac
driven to a concert
New Year's Day 1953

Mongol Mutt

And who cares?
    Not shaman bears or Chinese root-men.
All of it a glove,
    a turn of the wooden hand.
Enter trumpets across sage plains,
    eye-act over level lines,
black ink in blue notebooks, done.
    Active words dog-eared
editions, ripe type bulk tombed
    bends wood shelves.
Parchment crotch exposed
    with silk ribbons
hold old leather together
    as if again a golem
could be circled and recycled
    back into being. Yellow
vellum shadows: hill-folk
    hand candles back and forth.
Snapped line-snakes spark
    out. Speak up
on Ellis Island. Pedigree:
    Mongol Slav Lit Pole. Uncle
Jess in Minneapolis writes,
    "Meltzer's not the real
family name, but that's another
    story." Meltzer
a bankteller told me means
    "waiter" in Hebrew.

·

D. Mutt, Mongol mongrel, zipped-up
stabbed apart by occult stars. Eyes
at everything spare nothing.
Tongue rugs in its catch.
Not Marcel's R. Mutt or Nutt
but D. Mutt
doghead catch of the day,
his master's voice, de-briefed
who bogtrots kennel odes
with deft con's paws
shapes sawdust into bibles
into biscuits for the trickster.
Lineage, alas, lost.
Angel name erased in space.
Mongolian clods, shamans and tailors
hump and bump all over the world
and each mutt not Jeff's Mutt but
D. Mutt looking up
into barking sparks of doglight
looking for a home.
Snap! snap! Haifa cafe.
Hey, waiter, bring me another
anisette, and yet I saw "waiter"
as Buddha *nistar*,
breathing in slow circles,
opening clouds of inwardness.
Ah, so
what?

Hero in the Air

Hero walks into the Airport.
Steps on a crack. Bang.
Out with his gun. Bang bang.
Dead-center. Shattered mirror.
Stops by a newsrack to see his name
in type. Blood moves rapidly
across the tile floor.
Let others harvest the dead.
Hero moves on.

Boards the jumbo jet,
takes a window seat,
straps himself in.
Guides overhead air
nozzle to his face
still burning from
the Desert. Hums
a hero song
in pitch with jet drone
of a mesa
his Hertz stalled on
& an Indian maiden,
Jicaro, he raped
in a cave. Got
clap from her.

Over a map of U.S.A.
Doris Day sings "Yesterdays"
through rented stereo earphones.
Hero watches the ass of a stewardess
lie about love. Below
magic squares & sigils.

Wings slant, metals flash
in clash of lights, slice
clouds into rainbow spokes.
Sun tilts,

dips into a jade lake,
needles of silver rays
bounce off Hero's shades.

He orders a Mary
she serves from a can.
It tastes of hospitals.
"Born Free," 101 Strings in
earphones. The stewardess,
an orange moon,
smiles above him.

Clouds remind him
of the men he's killed.
Hero moves restless
in his first-class seat.
Raises it, lowers it,
can't get comfortable.

Hero on Land

Byzantine gold-leaf blur.
Instant gun pulled from
shoulder holster shoots
lightning through a Senator
's soft gut. Florentine
blood-founts stream forth
& hit the floor
Hero moves across
history shadows
in newsreels movies
photographs video
tape. The moment
in flash in slow
motion stop
motion. Again
the bullets break into
skin puncture muscle
shatter bones rip apart
veins. Smoke
streams up from burnt flesh
craters. Dead
hours ago, bullets keep
entering an image.
Eternity.
Hero's halfway home
before he hears his name
on the car radio.

Hero Rides the Rails

Hero don't understand losers.
Openly admits it.
—*It's a concept I can't handle.*
Anyway,
who cares what I think?
Hand-held TV cameras stalk him.

Hero washes up
in a chrome washroom sink.
Microphones. Reporters
surround him.
—*I gotta catch*
the New Ulm Express.
Tips the shine-boy,
flips a Kennedy half
into the air.
Flashbulbs. Applause.
Shorthand. It lands
tails in the black man
's pink palm.

●

Drinking Wild Turkey neat in the Sky Dome.
Multiplied images of a strawberry blonde
bleed into wheat plains passing by.
She sucks an ice cube,
wears a white silk suit from Paris.
In bed she talks of her weak husband.
Hero doesn't hear a word.
Losers don't count.

●

When he awakes, she's gone.
What was her husband's name?
Does it matter what I think?
Drinks a Bloody Mary for breakfast.

Hero's Mom

Hero's worn-out old mom waits.
Sits by a window watching railroad track
weave silver loops across the plains.
Once great trains bore down heavy on the iron.
Steam speech rich in future brag.

Now it's cowboys, hillbillies,
honkytonk tenors
sing through radios
of love gone wrong,
hard times, cheap booze,
ladies with elusive ways,
constant paradox
Maya dishes-out
into cafeteria trays.

Hero's worn-out old mom waits.
Wearily thumbs her dream-book down.
Nothing left to sing or talk about.
At night the wind
hums against telephone wires
sizzling ghost voice choir.

It's all a wearing down
like silver lines of rail.
A wearing down until nothing's left.
Mom's empty rocker by the window.
Wind parts lace Irish curtains.
Nobody to turn the radio off.

Hero in Parts

—For David W. Peoples

You learn how to wait
like a bird or cat and forget the watch
with its false future.
He waits for a man
with a key to a vault
where a box with another key
opens a drawer in an office
a file in the wing on the 7th floor
in a building whose shadow
watch-dials Washington streets
out into perfect lawns
wired for sound.
Men who belong nowhere
are everywhere
working for somebody else,
bitter about one thing or another
which nobody ever learns because
nobody ever talks. Rule one.
You learn to stalk
as well as wait
and in between
brief relief thrillers
read in jetplanes
scratching the sky with code
someone below deciphers
twenty different ways.

from: Lil

No she-demon has ever achieved as fantastic a career as Lilith who started out from the lowliest of origins, was a failure as Adam's intended wife, became the paramour of lascivious spirits, rose to be the bride of Samael the Demon King, ruled as Queen of Zemargad and Sheba, and finally ended up as the consort of God himself.

FROM: *THE HEBREW GODDESS* BY
RAPHAEL PATAI

To banish his loneliness, Lilith was first given to Adam as wife. Like him she had been created from the dust of the ground. But she remained with Adam only a short time, because she insisted upon enjoying full equality with her husband. She derived her right from their identical origin.

FROM: MIDRASH BERESHITH RABBAH

We all know Lilith
As she moves across our bed in dreams
Closet-dark forms
Close enough to touch
Myrrh caught in gold gowns
Rustle by
Music of a million cunts

•

O Lil
You dry fuck
Hump bump in an alleyway
Maya Maya
No way out of your nets
O Lil!

•

Once more Lil
reduced to a blind slug
moving down your inner thigh

bright white residue on scarlet sheets
you receive new lovers on

•

Lily in the valley
Turns the town into a honkytonk
Juke-joint paladium.

Cowboys
With goldmines in squinty eyes
Watch her leather Levis.

•

She-demon deity
lies on the sofa
stretching like a cat.
Small hot breasts.
Miles breathes "Blackbird."
She accepts
the hash and grass joint.
Cool fingers
dive under my pants
ka! ka! ka!
Screech of all
Lil's hungry babies
caged-up next door.

•

Lil snares another
wiseacre gob, stands
over him shining,
shielded in dark power.
Dazed sailor
hornpipes over to

Tenderloin bar, to
snake-tongue
Fillipino whore
's gold silver mouth
drains him,
sucks his spine
into sparkling dust
on Lil's eyelids
rise up starlight
in Mascara night
triumphant.

•

Me & Lil on a hill of gravel
where next week tract homes arise.
Skirt off, Altoon's shirt
beneath her bare butt.
A truck from San Berdoo turns the corner
bringing tools and workers
to the site we fuck on.
Her eyes hold flak of dawn clouds
fill with shadow as I bear down.
Her shining white teeth.

•

When I was 20
Lil took me down
Sunset Blvd
thru Jazz City
in a blue Corvette
lent by another lover.

Lil proved
it's a shadow-game.
My poems gown dark forms,

glove them
as they glide by.
She proved the act
ain't the fact.

Lil took me
when I was 20
on the livingroom sofa
after two tries, we
came in time with sunrise
over a cement-winged freeway
surrounding the motel.

•

Lil in her doorway
teenage Lili Marlene.
Red-rimmed Pall Mall
full lips tip lipstick
along the edges of
my root fills up for her
pink cashmere sweater.

•

Lil flies
by mention of
His Ineffable Name.

Flew
to heavenly lily patch
to squat
and pop out lilin,
some say
100 a day.

Stately white lilies
blood-splashed by
Lil's birth marathon.
Pink bright fists of
babyskin
yowl on the grass.

from: Lil, the Second Shell

Seed-bomb her brass bowls
Graved with Aramaic bad news.
Bang bang tommyguns,
Slot machine jackpot.
Demon babies pop out like crazy.
All with her shrewd eyes.
All with a smear of her red hair
growing wild over infant skulls.

•

Black Lil, Scarlet Lil,
Left to right,
Work the dreamer over.
Gangbang pubic fruit trees.
Fondle, diddle, dandle
seed-fat dumplings.
Pump the gush into bowls.
A quart from each ball.
Quite a haul.

Black & Scarlet Lils
Wing off into desert hills.
The factory's kept busy day & night.

•

Lil in hand
a silk-and-buckle song.
Magazine lady
coarse flesh
bruised by
harsh volts.
Red-painted
tired mouth
step out of

snug dress.
Roll down
black sheer
nylons.
Kick off
spiked heel
patent leather
yellow pumps.
Page after page
reveals her.
I serve with
bowed body.
Cunt hairs
airbrushed
nipples painted.
She catches my stutter
in brass bowls
on the floor O
ritual symmetry.

•

Bronx Lil
head of Lilin S. A. C.
queen of whips and chains
holds court in the basement
every Friday night.

Her girls ride bright red choppers
parked in the alley. Nobody
steals them.

All weekend
a line of men shortens.

No one's left on Monday morning.
Not even a stray sock.

●

They said say an amulet
or kiss a mezuzah
until the Shin erupts.
Daven until blind.
Walk outside blindfolded
lest she look in your eyes.
Eat pounds of raw garlic.
Rub your loins with eel tails
crow entrails, torn pepper pods.
Put nettles beneath your tongue.
Chop your right and left thumbs off.
Wear a codpiece wove of briar.
Read Torah day and night.
Let Zohar be the dawn.

●

Facing Lily Rashi sees
her wings unfold
block light from his room.

Pink breasts peek through
gold-white swan fans
fluttering like Sally Rand.

Rashi looks up from Torah.
Nu?
Not good enough for Adam,
not good enough for me.
Out, Lilith. Out.

●

She spends all day dressing for night.
She asks me to light her pipe.

We're married by flashlights
in a circle of raccoons.

Behind the wheel,
the radio's on,
I drive a machine of letters.

She licks my neck.
A cornfield turns mercury
our bodies swim through.
Law reversed at night.

She wants words only at dawn.
I touch her mouth with language
then afterwards move against her.

from: Bark, a Polemic

I ran one down.
Now car-chasing dogs
Cower from my car.

He was a rear-wheel barker
Chased me halfway into town
Day after day
Barking.

For what?
Dreamer.
No matter how or why you do it
You'll get run down.

●

Bark is what us dogs do here in Dogtown
also shit on sidewalks doormats porches trails
wherever new shoes walk fearless.
Bark is what us dogs do here in Dogtown
it's a dog's life
we can't live without you.
Mirror you we are you.
Beneath your foot or on the garage roof.
You teach us speech bark bark
for biscuits we dance for you.
You push us thru hoops
& see our eyes as your eyes
but you got the guns the gas the poison
all of it.
Bark is what us dogs do here in Dogtown.

●

It's what they teach in school.
Go for the throat.
If it moves, attack.

Mrs. Callahan in 6th grade said
To get ahead you gotta be a head-hunter.
Shrink knowledge into know-how.
No difference between smart ones or dumb ones.
Everyone's called asshole.

We learn after a while of it
How dangerous mind is.
A mine-field. Tread easy.
Minding the store is easy.
Not caring for any of it is hard,
Cracks shields.
Your flags & faces crash to the floor.
You gotta remember
It's the Ship of State that's carrying us away.
Not the people jumping off.

•

Almost there
crushed dog
slammed to death
whilst stuck
in hot bitch.
Both went
neither came.
O merciful God
cares not for
crushed dog.

•

I sent him to school & when he comes back he can
walk with me down any street.

•

Dog eat dog.
Can't you see it?
Everybody's got a bite on
Everybody else.

•

on a leash
in orbit
spaceman
free fall
wired into
master ship

•

on a leash
window-washer

•

telephone lineman
harnessed to a pole
Rover pisses on

•

on a leash
doin time
chain gang

•

on a leash
born

•

Open the door for the paper
milk & cottage cheese.
5 new puppies in a shredded Mexican basket
eyes scaled, root for tit.

●

Neutered spayed
Fixed altered
Stud & bitch
Walk around in circles
Trying to remember
Something like
What to do

●

We came & never left your side.
Your damned hands never stop grabbing.
All we wanted was the warmth of your fires.

●

Mistress is puzzled & angry.
"I wish they'd speak English. What are they
saying? I must have the secret."
    Does he know?
    She buckles a chemical collar around his neck.
    The circle spreads death to fleas.
    "It's for your own good."
    Branded for life.
    Arf arf

●

Dog who didn't know he was a dog climbed up a tree & hung from a branch by his tail, swinging back & forth, singing a song that sounded as if it were coming out of a tenor saxophone.

"Dogs don't do such things," a master said who passed by the tree.

He put dog in his place & gave him a name & a collar & trained him with a rolled-up newspaper never to sing again.

•

Dog stinks of sea & rain
lies before the fireplace.
Ribbons of stink-aura steam off his hide.
Out damned Spot.
Out.

from: Blue Rags

Invoke. Invoke.
Invoke. Invoke.
It begins to look Swedish.
Or German.
Her blond hair.
Her black hair.
Roots of her blood.
Perfume of cups.
Inner white thigh.
Soft silk hidden from the sun.
Teeth. Tongue.
Prospects of song.
Invoke. Invoke. Invoke.
Her bite.
Against night.
Pulls sheets apart.
Spine tangle. Knots & eyes.
Paper Japanese mask.
Her tongue pushes through.
A hole in the center of air.
Poems in her hair.
Nest.
Blood of her mystery.
Bloom of her history.
In her stars we rest.
In the dark.
Her body opens.

●

You do.
That hoodoo.
You do it. In the dark.
Or in the bright hot.
Palms & corked polly.
Scorched parrots.
Rum bubbling on the dirt floor.

Each cloud overhead a loa.
Shadow of your prayer.
Wicker knots.
Drums unhinge.
Each loa wandering until you voice it.
You do that hoodoo.
We do it. Apart. In the dark.
Or in the bright hot.
On or off the page.
A yellow horse tiptoes the vévé's curls.
Your sunglasses frame a falcon.
Rum bumblers drown in jewelry.
Oceans dumbfound the dancers.
But humble souls in white abide.
Hold the sun above their pure minds.
Humble souls in white clouds.
Darken as you leave the shrine.
Black-winged rooster ducks behind an oil drum.
We turn each other inside out.
You do that. We do that. Hoodoo.

•

from: Vav

Take me with you, asks the angel.
I have no place no name nothing.
I am Angel of the Void. Vav.
Laughed out of Sky Academy.
I have no shadow.
My wings fold inward as in a tulip bulb.
I am the flower contained. Held back.
Free me.

·

The Angel said it was everywhere.
A despair.
Shadow snuffers.
Spark suckers.
Rob screens with vacuum cleaners.
Power the quest that ends us.
Piled-up dirt & broken stairs.
Golems empty of angels.
Swords upraised. War movies.
Our blood. Spreads into hasidic hair.
The shawl is on fire.

·

Angel won't be invoked.
Ancient folios are not Yellow Pages.

One appropriate angel.
Appears in the center of a star.
In the center of a circle.
In the center of a name.

Vav whispers:
Diagrams, wheels, letters, stars.
Decor.
Keep the eye distracted from the visible.
Let a fool unwind his navel.
Soon the cord will end.

from: Face

About face.
How to begin.
To make a face begin.
How.
From top to bottom
Or chin to dome?

They say he can't,
You can't,
Face it.
Face the music.
They say you can't face it.
That music between you.
She hears nothing but music.

Words attack face like lice.
Attach to paper.
Music in circles.
She hears nothing but music.

Each eyebrow a seismograph.
En face.
Greek in her left eye.
Hebrew in the right.

I saw her yesterday.
In furs.
Grey streaked red with fox.
In a room playing Chinese checkers.
Very chic.
Art collects itself.
Look her up & down.
She leaves nothing behind.

She hears nothing but music.
Last night she was a fire.
Burning all the books.

Forests fold together like hands.
Words in each tree unpeel.
Race through the world.
Silk. I reach too late.
Incense of her shadow.
It isn't done with words.
She hears only the music.
It is faceless.
I am not there.
Music is all she hears.

Tongue.
Sliced into planks.
Between ryebread.
Curly-edged lettuce.
Mustard.
Stein of Ballantine Ale.

Thick instrument.
Speak before you leap.
Alphabet music.
Virtuoso.

Tongue in my mouth.
In her mouth.
Two muscles.
Tough whales.
Twine & collide.

In the beginning was breath.
Mouth.
Tongue.
A lizard peers out.

from: The Veil

so sheer between what's right
and will be wronged
let's say the Taiwanese couple
on stage tonight in their launderette
washing and drying clothing
watched by two teenagers
in a non-descript Duster
windows fogged over with
potsmoke, fear and talk
with one gun between them
and an idea to rob
not for money
but to knife that veil
between them
and the good life

●

In the hole he counted heartbeats
but got scared they'd stop
listened to broken pipes
under the shit-hole in the floor
finally read the Bible they give you
but his religion wasn't in a book
unless it's the telephone book
so he stayed alive counting
letters, commas, periods

●

The veil

existed before he was born
and between his arising
shadowed the world he moved through

reaching for dim forms he thought
brought light

●

It was perfect
and we're all good at our jobs
but someone imperfect
bumped into the gun
looking somewhere else
and all hell broke loose
but it was only because
we're good at our jobs that
everyone got away clean

●

The veil

the moment when nothing is left
no control
a blank
time gone
her kitchen knife
in your hand
in her heart
and a new life begins
in the old fear
running out the door
buried with blood
everything too clear
the lights
no where to go

●

How cold
outside and inside this iron
I nightly write against
on paper she once wore as bride
down burning stairs
for my love

●

The piercing

Sunday late noon
a needle through his thumb
straight through it
the thread almost laughing
moving in and around
what would no longer be
a fingerprint on file
sworls of skinweb pierced
torn open just a bit
and blood managed out like a sap
he sucked
knowing full well there was no snake
except in his head
asleep, mutating

●

from: The Art

Organizing these myths these trends these
traditions these rituals
this history this pattern
this secret this hope

Organizing these stars into one bright dot of hot
white light
As simple as that

·

Once
each piece of paper
on the desk, on the dresser
even on the floor
could be accounted for
there for a reason

·

It is easier to say nothing.
But recently I elaborated.
Yes, I told the reporter
My poems are often connected to one
theme or symbol, long, aspected.
Yesterday all I wrote were haiku,
short and final. No difference.

She took it all down
in shorthand.

·

Awoke to see the Jew upon a ruin
Upon the brass bed my body fell to pieces on.
Perched like a parrot.

I'm free of you, he whines.
Free of your bones, your dark hot skin.
I'm the angel all your poems could never be.
Look into my eyes.
What do you see of yourself, your words?
Walls. Dense and doubled. No door.
Now go on with your life and let me to mine.
Sooner or later the visions open up again.
A familiar wound
Clanging.

·

Cigarette smoke in my hair
This is the cafe.
I open my mouth
Smoke curls out.
Not a ghost.
A poet in the bottom
Looking up.

I'm sure it's the city
I'm a plant not a factory.
Return me to green.
I'll be okay
Watching flowers grow.
Let it rain.
The sky reads me like a book.

·

Noisily yank a failed poem
out of the typewriter roller.
My hair falls into the keys.
Not grey but silver
whose light

reminds me of work
to be done.

            •

It isn't fame or failure
just so many books to read
so many words to write
and the backyard garden is
Paradise. I could spend
all day naming things and all night
breaking promises.

            •

Dawn loon
silhouette
skims over the lagoon

its crazed song
unable to tame my rage into
a haiku.

            •

The deception of a new typewriter ribbon
gets him going another few years.

            •

The hunt

in the rain was a failure
her knees in the mud
his head hurt from last night
literature left their guns
easy to let go of

rain and more rain
and enough pain to keep them both
alive in themselves as cameos
invoking curses like bullets
like rain like words against nature
ruining their hunt

•

Some enter and never leave
others go crazy beyond paper
some know certainty in calligraphy
nobody can read
and those in between
scream as pressed flowers

•

The edges

where he thought his life extended
withdraws like fire-shrinking paper
and all these years his love was paper
his body in a vision resembled a tree

where his life retreats
a lasso knot pulled into itself
and paper feels like flesh
his eyes become embarrassed
watching it withdraw from his touch

•

I go through my body and out onto the paper
She wraps my head in white
My eyes burn to read
I can't forget anything

No word or face or silence
They go through my body
Into its streams released
From openings into air
Upon the page

How the world is gone
every moment we are awake in it.

Entries

Enter paper
as entering a stage.
Entranced gesture
lit by a wineglass
she rotates by the stem
to smell its promise.
Why enter her life.
To disclose or unrobe
penetrate everything.
To be enclosed.
Open my mouth,
let the bird out.
In her book
song's a closed cloud,
my life a postage stamp.
Engraving between us.
Metal, silk, rubber, paper.
Spider engaged with art
and survival.
Enter the first room.
Between us a wound in paper.

●

O bride O queen O young and old
rejoice on Friday night

Falasha as well as Karaite
await silk sheets pulled away
unveil her body touched by blue smoke

Zu-bird feather in the vase
and a new moon inside-out

O we want and we wait and we watch

even the last crab-loined Samaritan
rises up from garlic bowers
to enter you and sing of it
all through the week

●

There's a power in the soul untouched by time
wrote Eckhardt at the edge of a forest
then entered that lunary park of blood-robed women
rose-faced, arose from their perfume to see
a sparkling wheel lift up the puffed chrome phallus
through assumed alchemic clouds
parting to sustain remembered gods.

For God himself is the power of the eternal now
writes Meister in green ink upon her silver forehead
their mouth-to-mouth brocade's a gold delight
to Heaven's machinery without secrets rotating
soundlessly as in a prayer.

Eternity's now
scribed Dogman at her heels
nosing up tall white legs to sacred oven
and a moment later she whispers for another
perhaps an Egyptian
whose tongue is parted like a twig.

●

The war is in the words and the wood is the world.

JOYCE: *FINNEGANS WAKE*

1957: my eyes bleed black notes
into your blue bandana left behind
perfume enters my white poetry
cell filled with books and paper,
walls shot down with art.
Noon light through white-papered window
shines on white-washed pallet fit for one.
Sizzling purple coleus in red clay pot
embraced by grey bone-bag housecat.
Solo bluebottle fly hums closer
to a spiderweb built overnight.
None of us are in a hurry.

Notes for Asaph

Asaph (or Asaf or Asof) was
David's chief musician.
A cymbal player.
      Play the symbols, David,
each breath a chance,
a pulse-born change.
                  "There are no closed systems in nature,"
      wrote Bleibtrau, no
      sure thing in music, the poem,
      the ground we stand on
      constantly shifts.
We intone notes, black dots
on paper guide throat open.
"I am making you a spirit,"
sings a Chippewa on earth
in harmony with chance
the changes, chants.

      Asaph
fronts the Jerusalem Percussion Band
his brass cymbal clash in desert air
light off rims flash code to devout
who transcribe it from tower to tower
relay dance across the plains.
"Praise HIM upon well-tuned cymbals"
praise HER upon the harp.

      Glide down Nile in green harps
brushing bamboo fiddles
counterpoint of outstretched ibis wings
Mo's basket snagged in bracken, braked by weeds.
Black Queen hears a nest of birds
cooing for mamma and with her ladies
alert to signals goes to music's source.
Clothe him as we close systems.
Play cymbals, sign time,

mark lines with dots, do
service with devotion.

     Struggle as cricket
against cricket hind
a music made, let through.
We need only open our ears
our throats.
It passes through
like light as song.

Thelonius Monk dies
my 45th birthday
years ago
a Seattle dj
told me this story:

      Thelonius was playing here
with the Giants of Jazz group
dodged all requests for interviews
but I got through somehow & found him
in his hotel room lying down
his silence unhinged me
but I kept talking
& after a while
he'd say something
nothing really
a grunt
& I asked him
what it was that he did
I mean
what he thought when he played
some dumb thing like that
like what he thought his music did
Monk didn't answer
he kept looking at the second-hand
circle the electric clockface
on the dresser
looked at me & said
"I put it down.
You got to pick it up."

18:VI:82

—For Art Pepper

Paul's *niemandsrose*
I place in Art's brass bell
alto Selmer on its stand

despite
encyclopedic light
held & shattered
by its curves
the horn's silent

& the rose
white like paper

Darn That Dream

Darn that dream
and bless it too
        sings Lady Day today.
The sea
        two minutes away.
Walking home
        and almost run-down
by a redhaired lady
        (Lil, again?)
in her bright orange Triumph
        too fast around
Overlook's curves.

                    •

Yellowjacket
        enters through
open window
        bangs into
a bookspine.
        Dazed for
the five-count.
        Up again
and again into glass.
With an unopened letter
        I push him out.

                    •

Today's mail:
        Jack craves
a magus room
        lettered in fire
while Brandi
        's pomegranate
postcard
        from Guadalupita

•

Music holds the body inside
silver-lined clouds, Irish
linen around her breasts
bounce up & down to Earl
Bostic at the Five Four
Ballroom. Out of sight
how music moves
into history's shadow
dim at glass bottom.
Draw it all back up
through a tube of
lost skin & hair.
beneath jade skies
     decides to join
mud-clown dancers
     holding Heaven up
with four carved poles.
     Pickering's
kabbalistica
     Dylanogos.
Callahan
     's ground-floor plans for
Turtle Island
     Institute. And Jim
Willems wants to
     resolve
Christ with Marx.
Process sentinels.
     Words against
time, ingathered
     drawn out as
letters, as
     ashes upon earth.
Bark bark
     us dogs

crawl over lost lands
        sing down into
subways of maze,
        yawp through megaphones,
Hello Infinity
        Goodbye.
A million trinities
        divided,
bunched into bouquets
        tossed to the Lady
orbits our o
        -ccasional lights.

                •

A wet-suit haze
        hugs Bolinas hills.
Dew sparks
        in pinecones.
Black Crow squawks
        and is answered
miles away.

                •

Poets
        rubberglove
through worlds,
        bring back the muse
alive. Her body
        on my desktop
Lilliputian shaman.
        Tiny arms waving
rattle and gourds,
        bands of precious metals.
Draws sacred glyphs
        in the air,

sings me my song, she
      looks straight
into my eyes like
      flamencos do.

          •

Darn that dream, knit it
      into a cap of many colors
warms the dome
      dreaming down Elm.
Japanese courtesans
      conceal
their brightest garment with
      layers of lesser silk
and all is in
      the unwinding.

          •

      Bolinas plumb on
San Andreas Fault line.
      Earth laments her wounds,
crude oil blood-clots
      stream thick through
balding woods, breakdown
      hills torn into by
cows and horses and time.
      The land
slides into the sea.
      Fault man,
his constant lover's claim.

          •

Sun shifts
      so Tina shifts

out of her chair
     to another place
to protect her skin.
     We change skins daily.
Snake leaves
     a lovely exit shell,
looks back
     to what he was.

●

Birds lunch, grab
     spilt seed and bread
crumbs off the floor
     peck at feed
spread along porch-rails.
     Mostly Sparrows and Towhees.
     At the bottlebrush
a Hummingbird
     wings against air
hovers like a helicopter.

●

Locoweed
     puffed on plains
reminds you
     it's still here
there
     just around the corner
gone.
     Who cares
what anyone thinks
     anymore?
Keep your head in neutral.
     Wings might claim it.
Hand wash wool, loosen ties,

dye sky with visions
either straight across the bored
        or back behind the stars.
Bless it as you can.
        Sound it, ring it
through an unknown muscle
        wedged in skull's ivory bowl.
She's serving Breakfast Tea
        in Tibetan cups, drops of
wildflower honey
        pull into a gold circle.
Darn that dream and bless it too
        sings Lady Day today
so far away from her we martyr
        in a mulch of rotting
            gardenias.

        [30:VI:72]

Boléro

Ravel said to the music historian:
"Once the idea was found,
any student from the Conservatoire,
as far as that modulation,
would have succeeded as well as I have."

It looms up.
Another word
larger than a book.
Boléro.
Eyes lit like radio tubes;
familiar phantom.

•

She extends a black leather glove
my lips touch

her knuckles beneath dark thread
please my spine.

Remains of love
our garden re-arranged
sheets kicked away.

•

Your angel fiddles
Paganini's new étude
pouring over dark
retreating flowers.

Sunlight at us
where nerves uncoil
we reach the end.

My shadow
like my words

looms up against light
each house keeps lit
against strangers.

Inside your muscled mystery
one more second of isolation
I beg you.

●

Time going
my smooth chin gone
against her soft belly

her nipples awake
turn firm

our mouths upon each other.
Mirror

my face in glass less sacred.
Hot water steam from sink bowl

ghost
smothered in history.

●

You run down the street in a new dress
low-cut, ample
yellow silk of inner rose
in poems never begun.

Neighbors imagine what can't be theirs
be mine.

●

Candle-driven movie
repeated nightly at the shrine.

•

Either Ravel or Voodoo drums
or a Woolworth LP of balalaikas
Red Army bassos tromp through

yet always back to *Boléro*
her flesh revealed
while I'm half in
half out of Levis
sweater shirt sneakers

Boléro afternoon
in her widowed mother's livingroom

fingertips
fire glaze her hipbone

tongue tastes
touches through her blackness
parted lips of pink salt

again and again
Boléro

•

Held in time's fixer
lost to telephones
bien parado

scratch hits needle
castanets break the veil

snapshot
to be there
in the center

again

•

To Europe
London first then Paris
despite all struggle
I become a famous poet

drink Chilean Riesling
pilfered from her mother's pantry
Tilamook cheese
pumpernickel from Fairfax

travel Trans-Siberian to Moscow
mingle with Shamans in Mongolia
on to China where my books are best-sellers

chop her mother's carrots
scallions
her cherry tomatoes

en route to Kyoto to seek a roshi
back to L.A. they're filming my latest
then on to anywhere maybe New York
show her the old block in Brooklyn

watching the kitchen clock
her mother works part-time today
there's a lot to clean up

•

Poets of the world rush to paper
wipe tears off torn hearts
arise and wear the poem as wings

and if that isn't enough
the next record is *Boléro*

an alto saxophone
toots of lost Iberias
Jelly Roll Harlems
your spine's a choir
of castanets snapping
under a Dalí-blue sky
clouds opening like popcorn
filled with *paella*

O Maurice!

•

Another failed aristocrat
I puff princely cigarettes
Sobranies
filled with primo tobacco
wrapped in black paper
attached to gold tips.
Play *Boléro* for me.
I light your cigarette
with a Cartier lighter.
Your eyes look up through smoke
and despite my Paris swank
you remain sensual and practical
with a built-in contempt for
princes and other fallen powers.
But *Boléro* sweeps us away
restores aristocratic starch

parts your peasant blouse.
We whisk across Limoges floors
room into room
as ornate doors easily open

The famous modulation into E
which all of a sudden
shatters the spell of Boléro

my mustache a Steinberg
glistens with dance sweat
medals on my chest
spark in her eyes
now sinister

November 20th 1928,
the first performance
of the ballet Boléro
at the Opera by the
Ida Rubenstein Ballet

I who never dance correctly
yet in dreams remain supreme
faulter of gravity's whims
hold onto her silk waist
and in the movie
dip and bend and bow
the both of us as one
masters of animal magic

At the premiere
a lady, clutching her seat
cries:
"He's mad, he's mad!"
Ravel adds:
"She has understood."

The Red Shoes

And I woke up dancing
     out of bed past kids crying in clusters
     mine hers anybody else's
     piled up writhing howling
     steamy cracked windows
     stink of ancient diapers sour milk
     cartoon rat whiskers crushed Raggedy
     broken Fisher-Price homes
     uncoiled rabbits Legos Tonka trucks
     Pacific mold on windowsills
     crowing black green alphabet dots
     burst to spread and mark monk-white
     walls crazed with Crayola faces
And I danced down the hallway leapt over the dogs
     and cats hunting each other for food
     who turned to attack me like a *corps de ballet*
     but I was dancing and I'd never danced before
     music from all the radios propelled me
Into and out of rooms where my lives erased
     and I leapt into space free of sorrow or thought or art
And she pleaded with me to take her
But I said no it wouldn't work
I dance alone the radios are behind me
And she said will you leave me with the kids the rooms the TV
     brokendown kitchen nothing works
     muggers robbers raiders
     clawing at doors windows
     snipers vipers pirates
     oozing through old keyholes
     gurus prophets healers Jehovah's Witnesses
     fisting the frontdoor into a tissue
Yes yes I yelled dancing past her down the hall
Yes yes the radios behind me and before me
Music more conclusive than the sun
And I dance down Russian Hill into North Beach
     old nicotine ivory Italian gentlemen
     young Italian silk misogyny

Beatnik survivors tubbed in jukebox coffins
drunk on history and hippie hold-out
New Age hobos piss at the world passing by
bent over double in doorway zoos
And I dance past Broadway's whores
    tattered bare butt blushing with belt welts
    ravaged vagina overlit hand-held camera
    porno filmhouse aisles I dance down
    break moviedreamer meditation
    breaking through tough screen
    leap a Nijinsky onto a rope
    sandbag through iron exit door into day
Dance into City Lights microcosm feudal culture
Everyone's a poet but I dance
Everyone's an editor but I dance
Everybody has a book nobody reads and I dance
    down an alley into Chinatown
    attacked by teenage Bruce Lee mafia
    karate and .38s
    but I leap higher than Confucius
    who didn't dance from his hut his palace
    his systems of etiquette
I dance to the city radio
    chien shanai cymbal dragon smash
    traffic cardiogram
    chopped-off chickenheads
    trout scales scraped away
    crushed boiled crabshell crunch
    ladle day-old pork barbecue
    from stainless steel trays
    into takeout cardboard cartons
    white porcelain Kwan Yin cracks apart
    falls on marble Bank of Canton floor
    cameras on tourists like goiters
Everyone's amazed when I dance over dim-sum trays
    in black acrobat slippers
I need no food I'm fueled by dance

Radios are in front and back
        they're in my ears
        my mouth is a radio
        everything I see and hear is music
        everything I say
        everything is music I dance to
Dance to a mad speed-babbler's rap
        tapping like crazy
        Honey Coles hold your hat
        Fred watch out
        better believe it Bubbles
And no trace of sweat
And no thought and no art and true to each
        second my body moves over the fallen
        and the arising

                        [3:I:81]

Nineteen Forty-five

Can't tell You anything
    You haven't already heard
        Before I say it O
God O YHWH O Plutonium
      At tongue tip
          Taste hair of burning ghosts
          Noh play masks
              Whose mouth and eye holes
             Smoke from within
A mutilated chanter declares an ancient text.

Can't sing You anything O
    Supreme Ether O Supine
      River of Particles
Heavy with atomic waste
      Bends down this praiser
         In disconnected prayer
        Razor morning
          Opens my throat
First slice light
    Carves a city apart
        Carries it away in fire
          Beyond the fire mystics arise through
Chaste in hope to reach the end of language.

Can't tell you how wasted
    Devotional seed
        Bleeds from eyes
      Ash in skull
         First blast last sight
Night sky burns daylight
    This Brooklyn boy
        Tries reading secrets of

A-Bomb in my mind
    Talisman against history
Which is soldiers
Knocking on a door
  To take survivors away.

Brother

Brother died there was no choice
Brother died in bed a radio near his head
    repeating rosary news of a word world
    abbreviated fragments casualties stocks
    weather reports traffic jams sports equations
Died without thought of power
Died with a name nobody knew but we who buried it
Brother died devoured
    alarming what was left of his body
    bones shattered by plague and abundance
    tongue and nerves retracted
    shrunk by the touch of all of it
    too painful
    unmythic death
    no martyr brother died for no known cause
    slowly died before us
    we don't know why
Brother came home that summer stunned by insight so right
    it stopped him
    drew blood from his veins
    reduced him to a gnome bent over in silence
    on the bed like a peapod we let clean sheets
    fall gently on his body not to break anything
    it was that bad
    shades drawn then doubledrawn always night
    the radio repeating news twenty-four hours a day
    except Sunday
    when prophecy redemption damnation choirs
    made brother suffocate
    scream into rubberfoam-filled pillows
    his mouth tore at like a dog
Brother died there was no choice
Brother returned from war with secrets he never told
    everyone asking how did it feel
    how many did you kill
    did you see their faces
    he never told them anything

but asked about wheat and rock and roll
and stopped eating meat such a mystery
upon his face it froze there
nights the garden roared open
and lovers ran off in panic
mortar shells lit freeways
he wouldn't eat shellfish they were scavengers
insides filled with curls and ribbons of poison
Brother bought a Bible which led him to Market Street to preach
apocalypse to nobody
passing around him like a lighthouse
everyone going elsewhere
while junkies and crazies watched brother preach
reaching for light beyond ruin
Brother at full moon buried the Bible
wrapped in a flag of yesterday's newspaper
Brother awoke to shave his head eyebrows pubic hairs
Brother sat naked in the backyard for days
until hair sprouts like occult runes
reappeared upon his gaunt body
Brother marched with others into a city
and saw himself later on TV
in a cell a self-announced Angel
pulled off his pants
they had to stuff a sock in his mouth
everyone took turns
Brother lost count
basic numbers erased at the Bank
he couldn't remember his Social Security number
and when the phone was put before him like a blueplate
special
he blanked-out his home number
they didn't know what to say to him
not even the Bank president yelling in his ear
could break the silence of vanishing numbers
racing down the drain even his address then his name
stammering letters and numbers

memory emptying out
he made sounds they turned away from
speed-popping attendants clanked a gurney into the Bank
nobody blinked as they strapped brother down
four TV cameras memorized it
Brother the lamb repaired
returned to us in a wheelchair
a hunger to build a 10×10 shed in the backyard
paint murals on the walls
read through a stack of paperbacks
bought from a New Age bookshop
heal and return to life
all systems cleansed complete
blank page
ready and able
Selah Selah
Brother died we know not why there was no choice
Brother died in bed a radio near his head
repeating rosary news of a word world
twenty-four hours a day
abbreviated fragments casualties stockmarket
weather report traffic jams body count sports
equations child mutilation decapitation
husband tears wife apart
wife rips out his tongue
nuns raped dogs ratpoisoned
suicide club crashes rented plane into Mt. Rushmore
Church mugs State
Buddha incorporates
it's all Real Estate
electricity turns hair white
castrates twenty-two teenage boys
buries their pale bodies in backyard lime pit
birth rate exploding expanding universe
black blood drunk neat with gin back in Rhodesia
white blood used for sign paint
Arabs eat flies in endless marketplace of empty bowls

Chinese on the march 20 million strong
ultimate weapon carried along the Great Wall's spine
multinational empires sneak away to Shangri-La
the Pentagon's lowered into underground caves
turned sideways into atomic Nautilus manned by Capt. Nemo
twenty-four hours a day
repeating rosary news of the world
near his head in bed brother died
Brother died we knew he would there was no choice
Brother in his shed tracked words to roots
no difference between barbarian or wizard
one clan scales the pyramid of another
plants a flag into the King's cracked skull
Brother went with tape recorder to streetcorners
asking questions nobody answered
what difference does it make
nobody stands a chance they said
Nazi or Maccabee
none less noble than the other
Brother tiring
Brother wore down
Brother came home that summer stunned by insight so right
it stopped him
drew blood from his veins
bent-over gnome in the bed
peapod
we let clean sheets gently fall on his body
not to break anything
the pain that bad
burned from within
shades doubledrawn
always night
the radio on
twenty-four hours
brother remained silent
eyes open
until they shut

sheets soaked with pallet of body's collapse
died there was no choice we know not why
nobody on heaven on earth to remember brother
everyone takes turns forgetting
numbers and letters
forgetting
faces and shapes
twenty-four hours a day
I cannot forget

Brother died
there was no choice.

The Eyes, the Blood

What do I know of journey,
they who came before me
no longer here to tell it
except baggage of old papers
bound up and found in library stacks.
History's crying makes it all vague.
Was it myth we all came here to be?

What do I know of journey,
I who never crossed the seas
into the USA alchemy, no longer
anyone's dream of home.
Their great-great-grandchildren
jump state's ship, drown in void
Torah's too late to warn of.
Here *tohu* is *bohu,* America
another *pogrom,* another camp
more subtle and final than all
Hitler's chemists could imagine.
Home, *ha-makom,* no longer hope.
It holds light reaching back
from eyes watching Asians and Blacks
die on TV. We restore the shore
and our dream is gone. It
mixes into shadows growing tall behind us.

What do I know of journey,
they who came before me kept
what they left but now are gone.
Invisible shells cast off
in flaming hair arise
orphans of collapsed Shekinah
caught between earth's end
and heaven's end and what do I know
of journey, I a child when children were
murdered waiting on lines with mother and father
gone in gas or the flash of A-Bomb *ain-sof*

squinted at in movie theaters.
Ancients sit on stoops too tired to mourn
turning inward to blood rivers
mourning lost *shtetls*.
They cannot take me with them
and I cannot bring them back
and what do I know of journey
who never spoke their language.
The old ones are dead or dying
and what is left desires less and less
and what is less is what is left
and children run off screaming
Elohim Elohim!
into freeways filled with the starlight of cars

    CODA
My father was a clown
my mother a harpist.
We do not forget
how close to death love leads us.

I can not forget my father
crying in the uncomfortable chair
in a Long Island Railroad car.
His first and only son unable to turn
or run from a father's public grief.

My mother crying on the kitchen floor
a carving knife she couldn't use
against her flesh. Black metal
cast away. Broken
I do not forget

from these parts a music was once made.
She at the piano, he at the cello.
Late afternoon rehearsal. Slow
removal of light from the livingroom.

Discomfort between father and son
as in each other was the other
neither could forget.

The smells of her body in nylons
undergarments, buckles. The scar
across her belly. Dark fold of Death
the Angel's touch.

I do not forget
it starts in the blood and ends in the eyes.
A Bible impossible to read.
The rabbi I turned away from.
Kittens murdered in the garage
hurled against the walls.
Sensual hips of my sisters.

He died in Hollywood. Nobody there
to say Kaddish.
His common-law wife
a Christian Scientist
insisted no music be played.

My children will never know my father.
My mother will not see nor bless my family.
I do not forget that from these parts
a music was once made.
I heard it as a child.

Monkey

into surrounding truth linked by noisy monkeys—zoo-trained to dance around rock piles—grailed by iron railing grids—barbed wire—

Later that night in meat's abuse—unexpected tacky scene—

Going back on the bus—she's sure the eye against the glass—opening—was mine—a bubble looking beyond—spirit vapor—storm warning—cloud packs speared by Dore glaciers—grim Eskimos—bells and face paint—sweat—fracture lens—eclipse—dark days—before film runs out—

Lost gods—goddesses—godlings—godlets—of airwave wonders—ascending coils—other weights of light too spoiled to sing of —

And we go to the Monkey Bar to dance—to smoke—drink ergot nectar from Maria's garden of Allah—high on windswept cardboard Sunset mesas somewhere near R.K.O. Mars—a wolfen coven seizing spores between gold—chromium—teeth—

An approach we face alone as the poem divides back to the one writing it—I open my mouth before the hood drops—

Bruised before Yahweh—singing blues via crank-up gramophone—sand-blasted disc—racket of decoded time—I didn't want to pray: shawled and bound—twisting *tzitzit* around my fidgety fingers—Nous abounding—surrounding each atom—she sang—my head—heavy with inoperative gears—cognitive ruts—stuck counting tiles below—wait for needle to shatter inner circle which—when hit—trips platter's end—

We all began variously—to unwind—

Wanted to be taken away—or beyond—or even to be here now—awake to all of it—whatever's beyond it—within it—I wanted the works—the lights—

Free of it all—the vocabulary bussing through white spaces—dumbly served by life—fumbling thumb-index lexicon for new ones—indeed a bumbler—a numb soul in ink—nibs and type—dip cold edges into gray escalators—subway cars take me back to arcane books—I wanted transformation—acts and arts of reading—hurled back—in the grid of light broken by iron—cross-wired—back on thick streets—human air— sacred structures propped up—still secret—

In my monkey suit on Monkey Island—nobody knows whether I'm awake or alive—I keep my trap shut—they see me as scenery—back-drop kitsch—Rousseau—some barrio muralist spraypaints day-glo— boulevard jades—sizzle pinks—lewd palm fronds prod blue nylon skies—drunk volcanoes erupt dry-ice trays—orange rind grog— Maraschino cartoon moons—nose-down extra-long brown cigarette ferments in glass ashtray—

Suave in my tux—I hop from table to plateau—a tightrope walker through crowds—my thick palms—awake to the warm—flash of silver trays—I bow—

In my monkey suit on Hollywood Boulevard—singing in the rain— Kong gone wrong in spats—tails—top hat—a late-night movie—the god who is everywhere—a plurality of illusions—

"The monkey also wishes it had a straw coat"—worn in Basho's warm rainfall—neon pellets stipple her eyelids—too stoned to open—album-cover mouth moves over the song—eraphoned into her gelatin skull—

To ape my monkey bent—a strange range of events—finds me—tail-less—estranged on real mythways—anonymous mark—monkey-shining blur of signs—wall-leaning hustlers hawk codes—offer coke crack or junk—white way mystery powders—cooked or tongued—or tubed up the nose—fired into veins—kingdom bullets—lift the crown—beyond form closure—

For a moment—this monkey—slumps down—low—erased—

Now to know nothing—unknown—leap up—barefoot—throw back their garbage—fondle pecker—pull at it—

Gelobt seist du, Niemand.
Dir zuleib wollen
Wir blühn.
Dir
entgegen.

All systems want out—even ones that worked

Playing at light's other side—skin tattooed with *sh'viti*—blue and red—
letter trees—her black fingertips touch—torn red plastic fingernails—
down his scholarly back—

The past you accomplish—becomes our future—otherwise, no
wisdom—merely armies in the Name nobody can pronounce—

Outside: footsteps are apples falling off the tree—cycles of entering—
retreating—what is the world we see—cycles of seeing—where to go—
when to leave

It's a real tree my words mistake for light.

wood heart sound-board Bach Suite
No. 1 in G Major bowed from a rare cello
bow-hairs over strings hiss in earphones
Yo-Yo Ma where before it was Casals on 78s

wood heart of old Pinocchio
a cricket ready for death O
wooden exits my father bowing his cello
in an empty livingroom

all that's left is wood floor beams
behind sheetrock walls
doors, stairs, bow's undertow
vibrates soles of feet

heart's wood, wood's wound
music left behind for termites

[2:XI:85]

who's the jew where is he she it that looms up in your face unavoidable hiding behind the scenery manipulating agitating convulsively difficult and wordy

who's the jew on the tree bleached into Aryan calendar art

who's the jew in tubs of intestines and folds of eroticism overwhelming orifices with Wilhold sperm percolating metastasizing permutations of monstrosity

who's the jew in blood of shrugs and connivance pulling back the silken shroud sequentially breaking wings without regard for sound or pain

who's the jew on the freeway wheeling dealing and anxious to please to acquire taboo eliminating all competition

who's the jew inventing America

who's the jew with perfect anonymous plastic generic mask nose thinned lips blue contacts

who's the jew taking inventory of Taiwanese schlock

who's the jew on the tube with his dick in his mouth on overdrive plugging product

who's the jew who knew the waiter at the place everyone pretends not to be jews pretending not to be

who's the jew crossing the line of pubic hairs in mountain-range formation elephantine tongue roots and scavenges for more

who's the jew on stage in putty nose kvetching about who's the jew who's the jew in church behind a pew smelling of putrid knees

who's the jew kids throw ka ka swastikas at tearing away the
awning of a gauze temple

who's the jew he she it of corpses and grossness mulching
gardens molting meanings constantly overturned

who's the jew wormed inside brains expanding to devour words
holding the world together in a perfect circle

who's the jew shrewd ferret weasel alien darkness fouling
paper with copyright and power

who's the jew who knew you once when there were no jews

who's the jew you told secrets to

who's the jew we feed to history

who's the jew night gives ink to

who's the jew in chalk-white pies skidding into laughing death

who's the jew who can't say no but won't say yes

who's the jew talking to

who's the jew's friend

who's the jew to you

who are you are you the jew

•

old reds to this kid in the ace of knowing
old reds in blue prole denim workshirts
old reds following Robert's rules
old reds with thinning hair consuming huge bosoms
old reds met Friday nights in the storefront
old reds in a row on metal folding chairs
old reds listen intently to ancient seer red
old red sage who'd been there and back and saw the
        impossible
old reds talking walking utopia with oldest red
Comrade Lenin in Brooklyn on a fund-raiser

old reds in gold-lit memory reverie
old red fists clenched arms upraised
old reds arise against imbalancing power
old reds resist soul-gobbling machinery
old red hands coiled around sledgehammers
old reds skinny sinewy bony in rolled-up shirtsleeves
old red families picnic on worn park grass May Day fest
old red recalls Big Bill Haywood in Greenwich Village
old reds in a carnival tent hear
Paul Robeson back from the Soviet Union
his silk black basso pops out speaker cones

old reds discuss endlessly Talmudic
old reds want Harlem back and the Depression
old reds want unions back
old reds want to know what to do next
verify demonstrate form a study group exalt
oldest red with piles in British Museum
rubbing frenzies with Rimbaud in the Reading Room
while outside Industry's soot ghosted roar
bombards promethean cathedrals day and night
gigantic blood-inked paper rolls
squash books into stacks tongued through gears
of night terrors seeding momentous activity

those machines won't stop despite bodies stacking up
pulped by wheels remembered by ancients

in bookstores closing down
Party offices now boiler-rooms run by phone wizards
pulling the plug out of the Good Life
for all you material rubes asleep at the spiel

Millennial

it expects to be announced

no one has a clue
except those flapping floppy Bibles
in your face

even anticipating *something* is a tip-off

forget it
the vocabulary of travel
of getting somewhere
going someplace
arriving

it's gone before the hangover kicks in

whatever happens is theatrical, i.e., in obeyance
to the sacred script

who's coming for anything? even dinner?
the Messiah? Utopia?
trance-ending transcendence?
who's there? what's up?

inside a Tupperware globe cowl with punched-out eye-holes
whatever I see is what I'm looking for

doubt's the fuel that burns the bed with hope

an American flatness, an image,
extreme cartoon void of midrange,
a hologram paper doll desires credit, dresses and redresses

look forward to what?
more of the same, the sameness of more

look forward to what?
violent wealth, mutilating poverty

look forward to what?
progress returns to nowhere
where we find our stores empty or gorged with goods

looking forward looks backward

looking forward looks back to words promising a future
here and horrid

looking forward for words to work as bullet-proof vests
looking for words to eat

or really not looking anywhere
not even within
let creepy kids sleep

really not looking but seeing everything look away

looking away the way subtle or obvious villains on TV do

looking away the way one walks away from an open hand

looking away the way power pimps declare innocence
turning away to whisper to attorneys

looking away while evil disperses into the commonplace

in a rut of glut

a tub of electric fish
a glue of rust
in a glance a bullet breaks our spell
in a rush to future's past

in a hurry to score to intake partake
a moment out of time out of money
in a rut stunned by loss

nobody looks down on their way to pay
for play that won't stay in place
replacing everything with everything else
until nothing looks good
nothing looks back
nothing looks straight ahead
doesn't wince in blaze of lights
plugged into mini-cams circling prey
helicopters roto-tilling night
nothing talking millennium
nothing doing
nothing done

no one's got a hint but something's wanted
don't lock the door
keep walking away from the sound
pay monthly dues
sing shoeless blues
watch unused body darken
watch unused muscles soften with sot
watch unused kids fill air with death
watch unused outcasts blast glass apart
watch unused animals pace back and forth
watch and wait and sleep through all particulars
insomniac defender against all noise alien to dialtone

diversely uniform
class-coded tiered torment choirs
orgasmic cables lasso body politic
laocoon replay tears hearts out of beginners
cancel as many lives as possible
planet's going down the toilet
refuse hands eyes of the fallen

club all clans claiming community
dance in broken mirror workshops
tommygun therapeutic aerobic pillow-eaters
drown diving for pearl of self

what sign O seer
sun and moon laser stippled Happy Face eclipse
fussing over civility routines
suffering machines of debility
keep up appearing
step up with protocol
interact on oilspill
slip into interface
network coded digitalized hiss
locust tapping keyboard PC enthralled
what sign O seer what omen between the lines

it expects itself
it is already being denounced
no one has a clue despite piling floppies
anticipating rips out another row of sutures
doubt fuels hope
flat future re-runs
sameness of more

[1994]

No Eyes: Lester Young

This sequence of poems is a prolonged meditation on the last year of Lester Young's life. It was inspired by a photo in the *New York Times Book Review* section in the early '60s: Young sits on his bed in the Arvin Hotel in Manhattan the year before he died. Ghastly pale, stooped, he holds his tenor saxophone in his lap, his right hand covers its bell. The bed's made but somehow rumpled; there's a phone on the small night table by the bed & the hooded nozzle of the tenor's leather carrying case. Everything in the picture seems to slant downward. I've carried the photograph with me for decades. It's on yellowed & wrinkled newsprint, giving it a talismanic aura.

Lester had "no eyes" for bad vibes crude moves
abrasive invasive uncool imposition on smooth flow
sounds through smoke-filled black and white

Lester's retreat was away from injury
at times light was knives, her softness
his desire for flight

No eyes for hassle
brute verbal confrontation
rage fists knee gut slam jolt
to settle a linguistic entanglement
prefer a distancing reverie
easy fold into fold of sound against soul
cashmere

Defeat cap in mud
knocked off head
papa cowers from thug
won't protect son
from violence

You're in the Army now
a little Jew guy sings on stage in a movie
O how I hate to get up in the morning
Lester in the exile brig gig
cops a plea yes sir no sir

No eyes for disdain
pain of face of skin of race

No eyes to smash brains into cellophane
no eyes for paradise if it's ruled & regular

no eyes for outsize posters
no eyes to chew chump food on the q.t.
beauty not nourishment

no eyes for intrusion or delusion
no eyes for skin confusion
no eyes for diffused blues
no eyes no eyes

but eyes for guys who play sympathy changes
no symphonies
listen to my news
dues is truth
deep eyes for struggle
for flight
no eyes for escape

●

eyes size up every detail
seize silk curve skin delirium
dig impossibility as plausibility
eyes move through
you know how it goes
hydromatic fluid-drive eyes
click into gear & go

eyes to groove for the lamest cat
blowing pure heart
into clouds of shinola
ah eyes

•

eyes to hear touch taste blues gone
blues of the found instant recirculated
eyes for faraway cool dragon root China
eyes for big rivers carrying nothing but fat moist
perfumy heaps of huge gorgeous flower petals
riverbanks bands play around the world
all of me why not take all of me

eyes for prisoner of love me or leave me
eyes for taking a chance on love is here to stay
eyes for just you just me eyes for Indiana
eyes for all those foolish things that remind me
I can't get started on the sunny side of the street
it's almost like being in love
no eyes is blindness
no eyes is Hamlet skull
in cool Larry O black & white
not to see but hear
to tap tap ridges & edges
of streetcorner solid world
stand there blowing ride cymbal of coins
popped into tin baking cup I cook
my eyes into blue dream stew

•

vibe tones hair conk sizzle
they ask me what I do
a secret from all zones
into simple necessary breathing

is it sauce or reefer
works inside fingers padding notes
brass tunnel lady flower carved sworl
play pretty is as pretty does

do you do right

they ask me how I knew
what I know
how it works
open secrets

●

I look out for every loveliness
pretending is all I do
hide a heart that's blue
when the world's cold
discovered the story was phony

he ain't got rhythm
so no one's with him
the loneliest man in town
lowliest man around
what do I get
what am I giving
not the same as I used to be
tragedy seems the end of me
born to love
hiding a heart that's blue

so blow man blow
ofay crewcuts puke go go go
Bean states majesty
hip suave garbed in finest finery
bell to bell jump beyond blues
honky college kids
holler for honking

I look out for every loveliness

•

born in summer heat August 27th
Virgo a pure soul
nothing's sure but give way to air
despair coiled around brass of blues
who'd know how alone each sound is
chained to surprise
lies your gods nail me
caress me embed me in a heel of light
stomp down supple spine
sip fire's edge
hard soil clay fist open up lone flower
she pins to her hair before walking on stage

•

lady this & lady that
I'm the namer the sayer
up 'n' Adam halfway out the garden
chased by a rakey snake slamming the door shut
lady Eve whose day got caught covering up
her ladyness w/ leafy shame

am the namer not the blamer
hip to each word song hangs in air to tell
lady luck runs out w/ the bass player

drummers get nothing but leftovers
their kit's too big to pack in a hurry
I switched to reeds & touch every dot in your heart

lady this & lady that
like royalty I dub thee
loyalty scrubs thee skinless
winners losers bad cat bruisers
name thee lady this & lady that

Adam's spook I speak new riddles
cats scuffle what's he getting at
rats scuttle out of sight
pound your lights out
lady your name is death & love
a riff between the beat

I name like the clay man
what I say it is it is
what it is is what I say
is you is or is you ain't my lady

•

dig the paper moon full & dangerous white tonight
dig loose wig cats pulled by the tripper
do shit to other cats
cut up air with fast & sharp notes
dig how it all plays out
while I stay out of it upstairs
plop a platter on the phono & dig Jo Stafford
woven up in nylon strings sheer as first wound
wind down in the micro crack between night & day
you are the one in cold gray before warm orange
colored sky opens Broadway up to day people

•

don't like a whole lotta noise
eight changes where there oughta be two
ladies take it & run it back wrong
but cop bread in fistfuls
too much cement in spaces
no eyes for too much when enough's the truth

he's an old junky
he's an old funky funking & all that shit

no shit
no shit in my nose
nothing
I'll drink & smoke
ivy-divy

seeing's believing & hearing's a bitch
all the physicians come to hear the musicians

•

I was a kid in beat of open end days
the band rehearsed in the livingroom or in a tent
where tophat shamans begat blown glass bottles
of elixirs nostrums cure-all fix-all green or cherry red
hangover juice could hit limits before crashing
passage into death's shadow plays & shit all over
your head in a bowl
heave hallelujah

I was a kid in offbeat Baptist exaltation
hug everybody lift them upwards
beyond dust into big picture eternity
if you couldn't hear it
it wasn't music
it wasn't spirit

sad old cat in a flat hat no longer a kid
who reads the notes even when they dance away

it was smoothness man
no knots
great spreads of possible
infinite ease & clearness
through brasswork maze & leaky pads
amazing breath & space gone
each second it works its way out
an instant ghost

•

constitutional psychopathic state
manifested by drug addiction
(marijuana, barbiturates)
chronic alcoholism
& nomadism

eyes for bells & sweet dreams
in & out of nowhere bus stop town
drift on a reed
dread nothing but you'll never know
just how much I love you

sheik of Araby on a spread of sand going on
        indefinitely
snakecharm cactus into rose gardens
three little word blossoms sex red
fuzzy yellow dot-dot-dash misty pistils

oh say can you see PFC Young in KP bughouse band
uncoiled skins float in wet tubs

wander through blues & woe &
don't the moon look lonesome shining through the
          trees
sliced & dialed dealt & thrown on the table
a fan of fate the fat AWOL cat
reads like a book writ by star blotted clouds
chunky angels & red hot devils stir the stew

grays & ofays stoke a furnace
melt down Conns & Selmers into
honey poured ingots of eyes
spoons Tambo washboards his chest
in blaze of gold tonk
PFC cap in hand scout a shaded spot
anywhere in limitless seeking oasis
where the players are always ready

moon scimitar masonry
stitched into cat's fez opens a rude door
into courtyard dazzle garden
Jo Jones brushes blur in figtree shade
brass bowl cornucopia
brilliant outgush eye ache
water beaded fruits spill out onto white linen
Freddie Green sips thick black coffee out of tiny
          white cup
Basie puff puff hookah hooked into Buck's horn
cloudy ladies wait for the downbeat

solo out into smoke woven void
lonely not alone sweet & lovely Lester leap in
yellow ripple jade pool plunge her beige body
a fish in deckled light chips arise
with eyes & hands me a mouthpiece to suck in
          sunrise

Quasimodo bells tinkle uncorked navel of universe
no wavering in arising together a clatter of rainfall
spritzes the rest of the band in palm tree oasis

sheiks of make believe on funky hilly camels
clop over endless desert going everywhere &
        nowhere

                        •

I can't I don't play like that anymore
I play different, I live different
now is later, that was then
we change, move on

me myself & I dies offstage
turn the page back into dark
someone turns the lights on
them there eyes can't get me started
parting there'll be some changes made
tell the story

I'm a ghost of chance & changes
too marvelous for words

                •

Prez in Paris sips pernod
chimes like boo
loose in milky green
digs the scene
everybody knows his work
like Picasso or Leonardo
it's almost like being in love
city of love lights

sweet twisty streets
petals flutter down on
porkpie hat crown

•

one awakes knowing sleep's forever
a blue neon wind gets through cracks
a low watt bulb on the table means you're able
to shut your eyes & read the book of life
& hear audience roar oceans beyond
voices no longer avoid the erased face
in the mirror doesn't look back anymore
got a key to the door & the lobby's a slow show
everybody knows sleep's forever
newsguy takes bets on the side
how long before Prez slides out of the picture

•

when you fall into heaven do you land
on a spot where wandering stops
when you fall into paradise is it merely nice
like an awards ceremony or a device
to cut through grease & finally address
everything by its first name
equality a tapestry
gypsy fortune teller crystal globe
popped on shawl top tablecloth
author the next eternity on a rolled-out roadmap
where every rest stop is arresting compelling
heavenly sites are gold circles on a scroll
I roll with the road & flow with the going

when you check into heaven is it *carte blanche* or
livre noir or neither nor just one open door
after another & you can choose any room

champagne in an ice bucket
nice flowers on the table
or tequila on a mantilla with a pile of limes &
rock salt salutes shot glass rim with vim & rigor
or overflowing bowls of chop suey
pink with jumbo shrimp
hugged by glistening greens & plump mushrooms
served by ladies in slit silk skirts
buttoned in jade & bowed in gold pouring
the best gin berries conceivable

believe it
sorrow cools it in nomad's land
& kisses long as spring & everybody
sings sweet like Lady can't you see

when you walk out the bronze revolving door
into floor after floor of better & better
no need for names like heaven or paradise
instead play nice for everyone throw delicate
flowers in warm showers of coming honey
into a choir of fine ladies playful & sunny
in room after room where you never see blue
it's all umber you dig it's all a play of pearls
sweet pink pussy lips blow three little words
into goose down swords
stabbed with arrows Cupid silks our loins with
Eros give up the weight & freight keeping us back

when you walk out of the picture no longer there
in a chair by a window or edge of a bed
everyone instead becomes memory in heaven
blow so cool club walls melt
hot chocolate over all the cats in ecstasy
dig a one & only
& keep it going like dervishes
in one blur of fur & skin wins the race

over & over again
when you disappear
fear disappears with you

when you leap into space beyond belief
free of it articulate able to say it all
who's there behind the door
Johnny Deathbed or Jesus Christ slicing
oranges & pears onto a white plate
passed my way as an invite to stay
when you say goodbye you're already
looking to say hello to anyone going along
a road of light like lava angels tapdance over
& out jim it's simply zipped & done
with wings & mirrors

was there too in hoodoo's doing
as a kid & old man to dig how
what's unseen sees & what sees is blind
& ears straw it to heart
parts hot curtains to love's hot
butter knife slices certainty
out of the picture into melody
you never see but always know

when the maestros come back on stage
to encore the impossible
I'm back in Woodville being born
August 27 1909

•

men pack up breath in cases
carried back to rooms
they can't sleep in

pack & unpack cases
where brass swans rest
in between gigs & sessions
on beds of crushed black or blood red velour

a salesman on the job
men pack & unpack cases
to anybody who'll listen
get the glisten gleam of need
let loose in music pitch & itch to be free
want it all in a box to open
break seal after seal
verify a good deal in utopia
dope in a sea of schemes
on a paperhat boat soak up
oilspill & spiel
as fast as they roll out lines
& pull you in

pack up after a gig &
look around for anybody left
in the last note

dirty floors & doors locked until
tomorrow's grief
& borrowed chits keep me alive
one more day

oh pack it up old man
let young cats land on their feet
trash your past & praise you
master the moment
day breaks & coffee gets cold
outside light knifes beauty
pay bills dust on sills

owe dues
sing blues old man
younger than most

●

Von Hangman's here
in shit stained KKK sheets
knife picks teeth
wants my grief
thief 'll rip my eyes out
scandalize my name
when I dance wrong
to the cool
broke blue mouth

to die on a tree of life's a riddle
Von Hangman's been hanging
peoples before & after I was born

Von Hangman drags bones
top a slick black pony
snorts fire spark confetti
hoofs do dainty tapdance on copper sheets
blood path maps journey

Von Hangman's got B-movie eyes
battery-run red lights roll up into
gold cave brain skull
scrolls lists of cats
& checks his trick book
crows hook to his shoulders
Von Hangman counts each crop
with cool eye & smug remove
caw caw
always more always more

Von Hangman's a hungry sucker
who never worries about more helpings

●

what's cool isn't what you drink
drape or shade or lay back on

if you ask you don't know
if you know you don't ask

●

if exhaustion were an ocean
I'd dive in head first
& forget how to swim

down to the deepest deep
creep along bottom's bottom
& sleep w/out dreaming

turn blue in salt cold
shrink old prune gray
water filled folds pop open
on sunny days

no more sweet or sour
just hour after hour of no time
is nobody's time w/ nobody around
to keep time

if misery were the sea
& blues were sky
I'd still sink & fly
& cry w/out anyone
being around to spy
on Prez & say shit

the suit fits
the wood fits
the earth fits
dark fits
worms fit right in
& out & who's to know
who's blowing elsewhere
who cares

if blues were shoes
I'd walk a million miles
& still not be through
my map of traps

to run changes is not my game
chords afford hills I climb
in time to sing a song lambs lap up
& love sap fills the meter w/ sweet
hearts no glass fills

paradiddle tap delicacy
clicketyclack on glass bridge
over skin abyss drum
of slaves stretched
beyond break &
beyond kiss

if lips were song
I'd never go wrong
& stay stuck on your mouth
breath to mine in a circle of fifths

if blues were shoes
I'd be barefoot before I start
walking in or out of
your life

if blues were news
the dailies would take eternity
to get through

when I go I go there without you
through back door
blue light blink exit
out of frame tilted
solo in transit

just a gigolo a photograph
an 8×10 print a postage stamp
passport ID
out the door into night

what I saw & you saw
never the same
not even close
where I looked in
you looked out
saw only skin

was light for a colored man
was colored for a light man
nobody wins the skin game

bells bells bells
smoke a carillon
thanks a million
high beam eyes
can't see nothing but
atoms & ladies
move through
cloud shadow snacks
spines of light on shades
slides of reverie

in Speed Graphic clubs
booths filled with suits & skirts
ashtrays & shot glasses
washed in flash
through time into
shutter's petals

if snaps were real
nothing'd get anywhere
if past was future's fingerprint
love'd go nowhere
& if each note froze before it went
there'd be nowhere to go
if you is or you ain't my baby
I'd still blow words you couldn't hear

Beat Thing: Commentary

it was the Bomb
Shoah
it was void
spirit crisis disconnect
no subject but blank unrelenting
busted time
no future
suburban expand into past
present nuclear (get it) family
droids Pavlov minutiae
it was Jews w/ blues
reds nulled & jolted
Ethel & Julius brains smoke
pyre of shoes & eyeglasses
weeping black G.I.s
open Belsen gates
things are going to look different
when you get outside
understand that beforehand
this book doesn't kid you
& don't forget the third effect
radioactivity, the power to shoot off
invisible atomic rays
even if the all clear's sounded
don't rush to leave the safe place
Geiger counts light leaks from ash
hand reaches up for your eyes
yes the atomic bomb is a terrible weapon
BUT not as terrible as most of us believe

Tillich tells us "it's the destiny of historical man
to be annihilated not by a cosmic event
but by the tensions in his own being & history"[1]

EIGHT SIMPLE RAID RULES:
ALWAYS shut windows and doors.
ALWAYS seek shelter.
ALWAYS drop flat on your stomach.
ALWAYS follow instructions.
NEVER look up.
NEVER rush outside after a bombing.
NEVER take chances with food or water.
NEVER start rumors.[2]

Furthermore, acquaintance with addicts proves that "hypes" like being "hypes." They enjoy being a "hype" as a hypochondriac enjoys being a hypochondriac. They will argue that liquor affects people worse than heroin, that drunks are often noisy and argumentative, while all a "hype" wants is to be left alone. They dislike the social scorn, the inconvenience of having to hide their addiction, but they enjoy the effect of the drug, which keeps them from facing reality. The juice of the poppy wrecks the body and warps the spirit. The life of the addict is a living death.[3]

futureless clockface
Bulletin of Atomic Scientists pie chart
Eternity blackout
infinite unseen permutants
Hiroshima Maidens through
Saturday Review offices
shuffle bow hide mouth to Cousins
wrong & wronged *Fantastic Brain
Destroyers* "The testimony of a victim
will clinch the case against them
when they're brought to trial!"
"The house I live in, a plot of earth
a street, the grocer and the butcher
and the people that I meet;
the children in the playground,
the faces that I see;
all races, all religions,

that's America to me" sings Sinatra
in RKO backlot tenement
"A Kansas farmer, a Brooklyn sailor,
an Irish policeman, a Jewish tailor"
utopic plurality plastic lanyard
unity thongs for khaki G.I. nation hoods as
zootsuit jitterbug gold chain ceiling dancers
starlight all night razor & bullet flash
rationed gas & glamour
snooded riveters pitch in
to chance true romances
of misaligned diaphragm or
ancient Trojan pinhole burst
in backpocket wallet vault
dark backwards 4th of July
grope heat beneath cashmere
silk rayon buckle collage shields
stations of crossing over into her
nuclear August 13th rain of ruin
one bomb w/ 20,000 tons of TNT
evaporate mouth tongue ocean fun
red prong push back Levi pecker
from ache we sneak around parents
seek lava silk slippery finger smear
leaks out nylon rhythm crotch 'n' blues
Ruth Brown a humpty bumpty Louis
Jordan T-Bone Walker lindy magi
boogie chickerychick chala chala
"some of my best friends are Jews"
says Leni G.I. booted out of von
Ribbentrop's hill villa while Edward Waiter
Dachau's head shot himself
through the heart & lived to shoot himself
in the brain "He was a nice man, really"
said maid Gertrude of ex-boss Hitler
"of course he was mad"
"Claghorn's the name

Senator Claghorn, that is
ah'm from Dixie ah represent the South, son"
checkala romey in a bananika
ill at ease the little man said
some bread sir if you please
the waiter's voice roared down the hall
you gets no bread with ONE MEAT BALL!
movie swine sour kraut SS leather
skull pinups & power pimps smash up
Dana Andrew's defiant mug as
Great Artiste dumps bomb #2 on
second-choice Nagasaki at precisely
9:08 MacArthur stepped forward
removed a handful of fountainpens from
his pocket Wernher von Braun V-2
rocket wiz our guy on the range
cannibals all on the *Missouri*
always business as usual
population control & pesticides
Long Island kids grope out of DDT
bogs fog low flying cloud blankets
powder turns into oilslick evaporate
pocked skin pores German doctors watched
84 women react to their gas chamber death
"at first I thought it was simple lockjaw
a swelling in the back of the throat
light hemorrhages under skin
fever & a high pulse rate
rapid consumption of white blood
corpuscles, internal bleeding in
intestinal track" "stick-legged
starved bodies of European children
never smiled" "Census Bureau
reported last week nearly twice as many
U.S. citizens died of cancer during 1942–44
as were killed by enemy action in World War II"
"I am at present speaking less frequently

I have not been sleeping
I promise solemnly to the Almighty
the hour will strike when victory
will come to the Greater German Reich"
"If it is possible to outlaw the bomb
why not go the whole step &
outlaw war?"
"Two men
who don't trust each other
face each other
in a locked room, each
points a loaded machine gun at the other
one gun's a later model
no difference
whoever shoots first wins"
Picasso admired G.I. K rations
& Velvet tobacco rolled &
puffed by Stuart Little at
Ernie Pyle's funeral whose
chances were all used up
as cigarette shortage eased
"Yes, they're back"
Gimbels' sale of Army
DDT sprayers *Till the End*
of Time the biggest
noisiest New Year's Eve
bars open to dawn
stiff white shirt front back again for
chicks to lipstick write
General Patton fights for life w/
broken neck
auto accident en route to kraut field
pheasant shoot blood & guts
are we in time on time or out of it
college of cardinals on parade
red hat numero uno Archbishop
Francis Joseph Spellman of NY

Ray Milland lost weekend Anglo
Yank writer drunk marquis bosomy
Hazel Scott attained fame changing
Bach counterpoint into boogie woogie
"Mrs. Truman is the last lady" trumpets
Adam Clayton Powell Jr. contra DAR
earlier squirreled Marian Anderson
into programmatic darkness as UAW
Walter Reuther versus GM "They have
taken world millions they never toiled to earn
w/out our brain & muscle
not a single wheel could turn
we break their haughty power
gain our freedom when we learn
the union makes us strong"
"Kelly dances beautifully &
Sinatra sings the roof off "
Churchill Truman Stalin
gray trigger hairs at Potsdam
pulverized Mussolini hangs
upside down by his boots
Hitler shoots a tunnel through his lobes
& FDR's brain hemorrhage implodes
Branch The Brain Rickey signs Jack
Roosevelt Robinson "unlike white
players he can't afford a day off " B-
25 crashes into Empire State's 78th & 79th floors kills 13
ink UN Charter's ratified
Robert Benchley's empty Algonquin chair
sugar shoe meat butter tire rationing ends
the year future ends
Kilroy was here
read the writing on the wall
I, *The Jury Under The Volcano*
A-Bomb tests at Bikini Atoll
Five full-color Kodachrome *National
Geographic* bright blue sky spread

fed aching crisp nuclear white fleece
spine disc clouds up into Amanita dome
page after page of eternity beauty
gorgeous end of time & future
Vive la France cries Pierre Laval
it lasts only a few seconds
whereas fascism is eternal
firing squad day & night
can't replace the millions
Time reports shovel squads
digging extra graves for some
100,000 Berliners expected to die
of hunger & cold or commit suicide
Hirohito wipes tears away w/ white gloves
Vice Admiral Onishi's note to ghosts of
his *Kamikaze* corps "souls who fell as
human bullets" Chiang Kai-shek toasts
yellow wine to Mao Tse-tung
humble selves hate enormously
"one heart, one soul, one mind, one goal"
caped FDR at Yalta & death's round vowel
point over his eyebrow how the great man
shrunk into a cigarette holder at first
nobody would believe he died at Warm
Springs it must be a mistake
"take two" yells Joe Rosenthal
in the shuffle ripple U.S. flag on Mt. Suribachi
4-F bad eyes cameraman to
Iwo Jima icon Lt. Harold Shrier
Leo & Paul put together *Monthly Review*
on a kitchen table
will the world be able to recover
now that Taft-Hartley's here
& A. Philip Randolph's been everywhere
while racism slices *The House I Live In*
into frozen Birdseye segregated trays
Cardinal Spellman's red hat round face

wire-rim bifocals pearly pink cherry skin
O Christ your *sheist shmeer* on hot Hiroshima
pavement shadow clutter stained remains
evaporated finger puppet people leap Isadora through
DDT cashmere cloud walls & bop sock hop doo wop
Hucksters concoct unavoidable void
ENIAC cards in steel trays in room after room
menace of Russian communism
Mailer's Naked & 33-year-old best-seller suicide
Ross Lockridge Jr. Raintree's brain & Lowry
gin plastered in Mexico when Thomas
Stearns gets Nobel Polaroid in 1948
Baruch before Senate War Investigating
Committee "we're in the midst of a cold war
getting warmer" "I was well liked"
Willy tells Mildred who never knew Ez
38th parallel Inchon MacArthur 62,000
called up for active duty *Dianetics* via
Campell's *Astounding* color TV minimum
wage 75¢ an hour Burn All Reds
kids wear bead chain dogtags
Henry Wallace in Brooklyn speaks
farmer Yiddish to solidarity cheers
weekly rhythm & blues hits
charts top-ten tacked to SAC basement wall
Louis Jordan T-Bone Walker
ah everyone's apart
together
"Burn All Reds
No Mercy For Spies
Rosenberg Traitors Must Die"
anti-prole exploit flicks
"so shocking it was filmed behind
locked studio doors"
home front new wars
orthodoxy of conspicuous
fast car guys camaraderie

terrycloth seat covers mud flaps
hot rods to hell dragstrip baby
boom everyone's pregnant
military-industrial complex spending
arms production aircraft electronic
AFL-CIO merger turns labor into
management's chummy neighbor
on the way up to out
mainland El Barrio mambo
great migration to South Side
culture capital of black America
2200 new arrivals every week
blues clubs crowded slums
storefront churches sluts &
dope gangs blood cops
men fight fires
women in nurse teams
guys rescue gals drive cars
cats & chicks on Geiger crews
streetcleaning/childcare
police/hospital work
air-raid warden/social work
rebuild/emergency feed
Levitt ticky-tacky
white blue pink collared
workers worry about robots
racial mixing
TV's Jim Anderson
benign autocrat
calm cool collected not
garlic armpit Molly Goldberg
not hairball Reilly lunchpail not
life w/ Swedish immigrant mom not
Chayevsky's ghetto pastorals nor E.C.
Menace Vault of Horror Mysterious
Adventures Strange Science not *Mad*
"in the presence of comic books

they behave as if drugged" dear Dr.
Wertham Chuck Berry Johnny B. Goode
Jim Crow "reveal to white masses
Negro qualities which go beyond
the mere ability to laugh & sing & dance
& make music" writes Langston to
gangster nation Montgomery 13
month boycott "there comes a time when
people get tired," tones Martin
"history books will have to pause & say
'there lived a great people—a black people—
who injected new meaning & dignity into
the veins of civilization'" inner city junk
bebop & beyond jones go stone cold dead
sleep deep dreamless *nihil* no-go
Dreiser writes CP/USA "I believe intensely
the common people & first of all the workers
are guardians of their own destiny
& creators of their own future"
frenzy teens dance mindless
system's survivors in white buck Angora
sock hop perfect silhouette combine hoop
crinolines tight belt white sneakers
princess-line dresses black flats
stockings sometimes saddle shoes
what would Ethel or Molly know
when you can't stay or vanish
into gaudy frozen food frieze
or burn away in electric fire
shocked nerves dance
or vegetalized wives
lobotomy burns away
any real me reality
throw fetus downstairs
die in crash or trash
& draft terrorized guys
agonize on drugstore rubber

hose rites of Trojan warfare
Lenny's desperate Mr. Right
begs the little lady to just touch it
"touch it once" Hubbard's Axiom
"The dynamic principle of existence—
SURVIVE! The reward of survival activity is pleasure"
"The ENIAC computer developed in 1946
first electronic digital computer had
18,000 vacuum tubes & used 140,000 watts"
wait for the screen light to break into bodies
on a diamond or fracture jawbones in the ring
or contemplate testpattern's fact of being there
to see after midnight when snow or dark prevails
primal survive amazement durable trance
night sky to hearth to pixels
the fix is fact the stare's a given
vanishment isn't banishment instead
immersion in forget forgot for what
"Eisenhower's a dedicated conscious agent of
the Communist conspiracy . . .
largest single body of Communists in America
is our Protestant clergy," writes Welch
to Birchers everywhere & reiterates
Federal taxes a commie plot
whose ultimate grand design
is to reduce all groups & divisions of
American people into a mental state
where they don't have the slightest idea
of whom to believe or what to believe
about anything
Billy James Hargis
Christian Crusader
anti-com Minutemen
off to fight Chinese commies
train in Baja & Robert DePugh
trumps the bivouac w/ machine guns
mortars recoilless rifles

Loyal Order of Mountain Men Rangers
Illinois Security Force kid in helmet
peers through rocket launcher scope
Dan Smoot reports "The Founding Fathers
knew & Jefferson specifically said
a democracy is the most evil kind of government
possible" Clarabell the Clown
in Hell dodge balls of fire Jerry Lee Lewis
hair tendrils catapult w/ benny manic rage
arrogant confident boogie-woogie NRA
rock 'n' roll marksman how white sports were
except boxing hopes black would be battered
out of the picture Little Richard squeals & screams
"have you no sense of decency?" asks Welch
while Schine proves doctored photo
Cohn murmurs "threatening to wreck the army"
smears against windscreen smash summer bugs
pulp polka dot pus blots rush to get gone
young at 56 Justice William O. Douglas rules
segregation's unconstitutional Oppenheimer's
security clearance denied "fundamental
defects in his character" advances in color TV
where's the heart part the hope thing the telos
zing on No-Doz zonk speed to night's finale
in another zippy car on conveniently empty
highway back into a city to sleep the day away
25-foot neon chorus girl Hotel Sahara Las Vegas
Mau Maus Miltown Martinis & Viet Nam names
the 50s & 60s Chou En-Lai beflowered by Nehru
at Rangoon Britain departs from Suez Ho Chi Minh
Bien Phu Nasser topples Naguib & the Jabès clan
flee to France where *Juif* means exile & other
nation-states war to hold each border inviolate
violence either silent or loud backroom old sclerotic
erotic fuck feast jam all holes w/ worn-out elite meat
Jackie Gleason Loretta Young Red Skelton Herbert
Philbrick I Led Three Lives fink in Richard Carlson mask

Martha Raye Arthur Godfrey fires Julius LaRosa
"loss of humility" a disability in the new age
Billy Graham in London converts 34,586
electron microscope enlarges specimen 200,000 times
goes deeply into certainty's textures
atoms smashed into minuscule energy beads
throne of thorns crown Walt Disney's four
54 Oscars & it's curtains for O'Neill as Marilyn
weds Joe DiMaggio & June Haver returns
from 7 convent months to marry MacMurray
Shaver Mystery moves from *Amazing to Fate*
Bixby's "It's A Good Life" we work out of a
ghostwriting agency on Sunset UFOs in the hills
Orfeo Angelucci met spacemen in Greyhound
bus terminal met Lyra & Orion ah *Orphée* really
Neptune of the New of "eternal youth eternal spring
eternal day" "Americans feel they are the most
insecure people on earth . . . a compulsive need to
consume . . . no culture . . . no souls . . . much more
than their just share of the world's goods . . ."
"The business of America is business"
Urantia says in 1955, "It's a great blunder to
humanize God except in the concept of the indwelling
Thought Adjuster . . . The adjutant spirits are the sevenfold mind
bestowal of a local universe Mother Spirit . . .
which belongs more appropriately to the story of
your local universe of Nebadon" "Only one
person in all humanity of whom God has one
picture & that is His Own Mother . . . Most of us
are a minus sign . . . but Mary is an equal sign," writes
TV's first televangelist Fulton Sheen "Before taking
unto Himself a human nature, he consulted with
the Woman to ask her if she would give Him *a man*"
"Once God is dead & man is deified, man
is even more alone & estranged from himself
than ever before . . . *homo hominis deus,*"
Vahanian writes "your earth would have been

a garden of joy . . . a garden of everlasting desire
to serve . . . but man's lack of understanding
destroyed the harmony of being on Earth . . . he lives
a lost soul," says another master to Adamski
"a demoralized country neither rebuilds nor
recovers . . . social institutions disappear
skills are lost, knowledge recedes & the pull
of a dark age descends on increasingly ignorant
& suspicious people unable to cope w/ a hostile environment . . .
created by a nuclear disaster."

Notes

1. "The Power of Self Destruction" by Paul Tillich in *God and the H-Bomb,* edited by Donald Keys. New York: Bernard Geiss Associates, 1961. Page 24.

2. *How to Survive an Atomic Bomb* by Richard Gerstell. New York: Bantam Books, 1950. Pages 138–139.

3. "The life of the addict is a living death." From a tract published by a Christian publishing house c. 1958. There was a mammoth hypodermic needle on the cover.

Shema (1982)

Adonai angel wings
dark bandages float down
upon Your holocaust
O genocidal Maker
shroud them in one fire
filled Torah returned to
Angels unable to read
Aleph-Bayt
speechless
no word
no name

●

sense-jammed assassins
hang out of helicopters
killing shadows below

imploded silencer noises
fall like apples

up fly white-eyed bluebirds
through smoke columns of bullet holes
released by death

●

How to know the Name
or claim its letters sacred
when Zion's soldiers Uzi one
too many of the ten
Signs taught to be Law?

●

Dead parts hauled out in wagons

some open-eyed
shadow of her indefinite face
against another's hipbone
reaching up for death

wheels rattle
and bones press deep
on dark weight
vermin shuttle through

scythe of hair
cuts wax mask apart

cut-out paper crows
perch on telephone wires

no rite
and no more writing

wheel stuck
momentarily against
one who fell off

•

No Zion
and Jerusalem's inside
like a portable heart
easily reduced to four
diamonds once a name

•

Peel pages from the apple still red
with Aleph seeds blood-gorged
its stem's a grenade pin pulled out quick
tossed into the ark of covenant
exploding bloody apples everywhere

dead empty bodies on sidewalks
random letters without a word to form

●

word-formed meat
war's fast food for
crowned dog
and flies are vowel-points
upon their flesh
mark and tune
our psalms to You

●

Each word the word creating
protecting life

all else like bayonets
goes against it

in death's ink sit soldiers
wrapping dead in book pages

the book weeps black blood
in their mouths

the book weeps white nerve flames
thread sewing dead eyes shut

the book weeping itself empty of words

the book a powder like ash of bones
warriors paint their faces to attack children

each word the word creating
protecting life in lights of song or silence
all else goes against it

Shema (2004)

O Father
Do you not see encircling danger?
How is it our house has vanished
Without a trace?
Why hasn't my mother returned? How strange!
Has she taken a taste to travel?
I don't think Jews will ever be
fully accepted until we're Christian
just like blacks will never be accepted until they're white.
I work as a freelance self-hater.
Malkuth denied
Shekinah denied
Shabbat destroyed
In unrolled fire of Torah
Unknowable violence of EL
In charge of mindlessness

One day the language
will turn against its own speakers

The power of the language is
hidden within the name
its abyss is sealed therein

This is the God that hides
that everyone sees in a book
that hides in blood
released from broken hearts

This is a blind book
not the body shattered by belief

Unseeing letters are bullets
& missiles

Visions of the Apocalypse
- Made Simple and Understandable
- A Unique Public Presentation
- Open To All

in the passage
way away from
sea, the light
takes hold of all
hands can touch
& toss as bombs
into the dark
ahead & behind
Shema

breaks open the door
dead rat on doorstep
ants pouring out of his eyes
half-opened mouth
Sharp teeth in grateful smile
Shema

in dark bomb light
shatter vessels

will to die

impossible to mend

unite in light's metals
melting into flesh

praise to the One
to whom our praise is due
now & forever
creator of day & night

all embrace
life's lights
of death
entrapment's
cowl blackness

we believe more than we know
& know more than we believe

Unending is Your love for Your people
the House of Israel
Torah & Mitzvoth
You have taught us
laws & precepts

day & night
reflect on them
they are our life
the length of our days
Your love
never departs
from our hearts!

I woke up in ruins
what remains resists grasp
blood saturates all it touches

evidence external
conceals what's w/in
shatter networks
skin layers in instant
corruption of metals

praise who or what or why
green stalk unfold
or mold spot spores
flower in the heat

& mix w/ death life
life death the emergency
strapped w/ plastic explosives
allusive instant of amazement

we're dead anyway
either way

to die beyond w/in our
imagined boundaries
all for the infernal Eternal

Praise the Eternal
Sovereign of
the Universe

the kids skid out of lens line
smash into unending love for Your people

who are they
whose people
are we

Let the reign of evil afflict us no more

the dot drops out of sight
no elegant turn no swift recoil
we're bereft beyond words
& words are all we're left with

You alone
are God

Praises
Eternal
GOD
Sovereign of the Universe

in the rocket's red glare
missiles bursting concrete
hives of tradition

However much the Jews adapted themselves,
in language, manners,
to a large extent
in the forms of religion

to the European people among whom they lived
the feeling of strangeness between them &
their hosts never vanished

This is the ultimate cause of Anti-Semitism
which cannot be got rid of by well-meaning
propaganda.

When the EVENT will occur
none will deny its occurrence;
it's abasing & exalting
(*Surah 56*)

diacritical marks
deep sutures of
quotation marks
scar outflow
clot it, stop it

tattoo lips w/ deep blue
Arabic & Hebrew letters
stitch them shut
despite blood syrup

straining through the seal

You alone are God

We divided the Quran into sections
to recite to others
gradually

Believe in it
or believe not

Happy are those
who dwell in yr house
they will praise Your Name
forever

loops that knot the wrapped pharmakos
in spider bag over death roiling waters
sing glory & forgiveness
sacrifice is honor
loss is gain
stockpiling death mulch
life feeds on

no more note taking
notation
walk the 16th Street corridor
between Valencia & Mission
madhouse bedlam
unsprung *ursprach*

woman on bicycle
pulled by a leash
screams at Ramon to
fuck off I'm not a dog

dope zombies bond
move inward towards the score

loud whispers about the motherfuckers
making fools of all of us

We did not create the skies
& earth
& all that is between them
but w/ the Truth
& for a fixed term
(*Surah 46*)

bury flight in dunes
in mud in tar

Allah hears & knows everything

Happy are those
who dwell in Your house

Who is like You, Eternal One?

We gave Moses the complete Bible
for the righteous
explaining everything in it
as a Guidance & Mercy

sent down through the faithful Angel to yr heart

•

there were words afterwards

succulent hybridized grapes
seedless & stemless

The Messenger is a warner

The great event is coming soon
& none except Allah knows its hour
May we lie down this night in peace
& rise up to life renewed

O God
& let a time come when
morning brings no word
of war or famine or anguish
a time of happiness
contentment & rest

•

Allah hears & knows everything
All rise
ancient trees
silent
in deep dream
of roots & routes
that connect as they disconnect
no tradition but
tradition which
icepicks my eyes & I
am moon & sun to my beloved
blinded as she is by her own image
in mirrored hallways
all wrong

baruch ataw Adonai

•

"There is no cure for death
Not even health"
writes Rosenzweig
in struggle w/
midst & mist & the mitzvah
of resistance & reception

"Paralysis finally stops all movements of limbs"

the struggle is always to be
all of us
together
no division
separation or
false throne

real & ecstatic
it unreels beyond the screen
the dream
into the delirium of awakening

baruch ataw Adonai
may the One who causes peace to reign
in high heavens
cause peace to reign among us all

The insane ain sof aur rite as sleepwalked by Rebbe Yaakov Yosef ben Ariel as charted & diagrammed by Rube Goldberg & framed by Henny Youngman

Left the old country pronto & presto
am in a Lower East Side kitchen lighting
yartzheit candle inside thick glass
whose flame warms winter cold hands
wonderland I slip away into reverie
everybody tells me is meshugenah
they come for you w/ butterfly nets
handball your bod against brick wall pow
hicks from sticks hose down meat debris
Pet Milk splatter trickles down to ants
pant up god nectar glub glub suck sugar
fire through candystripe straw whose curves
caked w/ coke stoke other hungry ones
abundance beyond grip whose light stuns
turns shadow into silhouettes stuck on velour
jailed in glass case tray collectors pay to rescue
your erased moment & they pray at dawn & day & night
flutter nickelodeon daguerreotype sepia
powder flash Riis hovel real tzaddikim pick edgy lice from oldworld
    beards
what's weird's everyday
so pray pious remote
steam engine tracks take pilgrims back to pogroms
rags chickens & goats hide litters from beards
rage rite honed knives spark aleph-bayt up
chimneys into clear sky scroll cold as ice
leaks through wet basement walls
bodies stacked on stench shelves seek heat
thermal rot flora rats gobble blood soup seepage weep
winged Torah in her castle coffin cave
her unseen seas blind our eyes strain
born to see captivity incise its vowel points
into throats unable to sound street Arab
kvel at dawn in spawn of bug pluming room walls

whose paper flowers powder
snow bowers on cheder boychiks
Talmud deep immersion in old scroll rolled
into sand-dancing kakers holy machers
tumble into cantillated bramble lost-not-found
tied to stacked serif tracks guide
eye through closed text decks stacked lines
follow through time auld angst Dasein looped & fixed to read chaos
    back on track
allow the narrowing focus nickelodeon hocus pocus locus to plush
    lush flesh
cushions of meaning flourish even out
of breath w/ emphysema from cigars &
Old Golds alter gelt gefilte fish dead weights
fill lungs w/ Atlantic & Liggett & Meyers
fluids acids & corrosive pleasures
measure it all out in painkilling eyedropper
plotz on the spot dots on the lungs the liver
oy boys & girls the melodrama of poetry
versus body's telegrams versus spirit's
shmoozing mit shpilkes shpritz this
twist of fate's challah some shtoonk
infidel lives to tell while the rest of us
pour through a sieve of grief & absence
abiding presence of familiars am absolved
resolved & solved in salt's burn evaporate
lyric strategies into shrunk effigies
gevalt the vault's stuffed w/ loot
nobody can lift mit cajones burst
& worse & why do we dance & why
does yiddle mit fiddle know squat
about what kids jitter to
rave in ecstatic robotic tendons
extend beyond death trap snap off your feet
chop out your face blended into
frieze of frozen campers panicked
disoriented want to be in truth stables

achtung mein kopf certainty's skirts
drag through blood red dirt ash smudge mashed baby fragment
blood tracing rainfall tumbles down barbed wailing wall guards
go pit bull ferocious beyond reason vayzmer
inhuman speechless
whatever's a Yid must be gotten rid of
blinded by the seen desired hated ones bone particles
remain to remind
of unresolved fascination
ver veyst?
the Skulnick in hand
alas poor schnorrer
unknown golem
solemn isolate
in charge of nothing
book-driven mute
shtarker cyborg
kraut mit out bubkes
got no one to kiss
walking mud pie
yearns not to die
but to heat up within your skin
am a pisherke sharing sweet secrets
tongue each crownlet
each vowel point
deepen black ink
w/ pubic scour brush
bare each page
can't keep me off stage
kish mir in toches
no biz like Shoah
no wiz like odds
you can't control death
or dice in Bugsy's mitts
mit gelt he's a gone son
a gantser mach spun off the Strip
into yenne velt what's left

a sequin kippah
a drip-dry suit punctured
bullethole sieve
vayzmer
alien pain margin
nudges greenhorns into the new world
jazz compañeros
out of throes
unbound worker bodies
boogie Lindy shimmy shake
alte kakers veil shock lace
masks in cafeteria covens
musks through nomenclature armature within black dresses arise
gezunterheyd
her beard's sex cologne
pulls his putz
denture trapped gum meat
picaresque? forget it
bodies stack up in a mud trench
our striped bones dig deeper
everyone's next no favorites
death's chosen ones
let's be blunt
Jew's the one
Yid goes first
poet or not
Kike's the Nike missile
aim for its nose
its feet its curved spine
vermin bouquet pus
of infected stigmata
Oustjuden its voice
overt covert schmaltz
grease buried deep
in unwashed blackness
"fed w/ the same food,
hurt by the same weapons"

fool's clown the stray
dogs set upon & boots
goose & bruise & on the loose
phantasms smear ecto blood drool
over bubkes billboards
swords of ground round kishkes
red dred worms spill out stainless
steel holes onto labial-pink butcher paper
taped shut w/ ivory tape licked on one side by
hairy brush dispenser

from: Reds vs Feds

old commies look down at shrunk wieners
once hammer sickle furled off hot red poles
telegraph hope spurt code pronging & longing
for release & relief a sheaf of official documents
erupt up into the sky before feathering down
upon bewildered hats

      •

history's melancholy, I love you all
you'll die before any of my epics are finished

      •

in the slammer w/ the others
whispering triumph in meat slicing moonlight

      •

when are we gonna blink thick glued eyes wide open to electricity's at-
omized phantoms, sirens sucking juice from brains curving inward into
a fine black dot when the plug's pulled out

when are we gonna get smart & stop playing dumb

      •

when the revolution came nobody went instead
stood there watching replays on TV looking for
their faces or those fallen under horsehoofs & bullets & gas
& festive chaos wet with blood & hollering

      •

revolting sleep in doorways
bunk down in dumpsters clank the lid down
shut out stars & cop lights

•

cop outs & black outs
w/out & out of it
where the next edge makes its ledge
we leap out over into
your face & smash
subtle tangles into easy mush
oh so many wd be anybody but me
gevalt blast the vaults
smash rates down so everybody wins
that ain't no sin that ain't no pipe dream
I ain't no hophead puffing utopia
real deal comrade if we pull together
we can knock 'em off their pins
the whole of it tumbles down
like a pyramid of dumbo clowns in pinstripe suits
Monopoly stooges fall flat on fat asses
ask anyone with grudge burns
thick fingertips touch tender faces
with easy aces
let's win for a change, let's change the odds

•

hey May Day & nobody's on strike
nobody's on line waving red banners overhead
down streets curbed w/ flowers & families
falling in line to day's end to sway as one
in union halls singing hymns of muscle
bunched in solidarity above bald boss domes

hey May Day nobody's anywhere on parade
except some sad sacks afraid to open doors to
more confusion profusion of signs & lines so
twisted the maze goes corkscrew into brains out
of order anyway no matter which you go you
wind up at the end of another line
fists deep in dust

•

hey hope peddler sell me another hit off your bong
I'll sing you a song of breaking through to truth
gone by so fast the uprising'll be overturned
we're out of time before you hear how great it was
revolt's the moment
before form falls back into place
& floor planks ascend
ladder growing to the topmost where no hands reach down
to pull anyone up

want to be in that moment when time collapses into action
without past or future
breaking through

•

yeah time marches all over us tromp tromp
old reds turn out young ones w/ reckless unfocus
good for grunt work & utopian gumbo gab
old reds sink deep in time pile get stiff
some say paralyzed w/ nostalgia & what if

•

all those Sovfoto airbrushed Lenins & Stalins
workers hand-painted health vodka cheeks
Artkino color war movies noble soldiers

pitchfork peasants fight fascism
International Publishers books in the CP/USA bookstore
watched across the street by Feds taking pictures
LYL kids en route to a hootenanny *viva la quince brigada*

•

you got these old guys once young
sitting around a ruined table
smoking & drinking schnapps
as if tomorrow it'll happen
as if everything's in place

•

chrissake we need shtarkers like Mike Gold
fearless & loud
not young brains stained inert stuck in theory misery
while history mows down the lawn
rolls over the yawning
pulls the lid down
bulldozes soil up & over
cities & citizens
never waking up anyway
even when you push them or
stick a word in their trance
they say have a nice day
inside but no
light lets you live any way
the square unaware way unprepared to part ways
stay stuck tuned on freeways
heading out to fort home
in lonely abundance dance
to plants needing water

•

give it all to robots
chip-driven machines
in factories free
of human bodies outside
spare changing
picketing for cameras

•

storm the fucking Bastille
get real folks
as you get poorer
& the rich get richer
beyond need or greed
stop taking shit
fuck true grit
kick ass & break the spell
hell ain't less it's more

•

she gave up on me
you think too much she said
you vacillate which I thought meant
no balls at all while she stood tall
eyed-down bulls & scabs & took her lumps
but I had too much to figure out
she made my number & gave up

•

he quit on me
you're stuck in committees
bolsheviks atrophy in
office mazes & hives
clack chat on the Nyet

he said you're dead
you're nowhere near the barricade
you love paper too much
you're too afraid to do much
except dictate memos to temps
your drone slows to stupor

•

they quit it & moved out
to mall control exile
comfort & anonymity
a tragedy their years of revolt
lay buried beneath astro turf
while worms work through
glued eyes
paradise of affordable paradigms
shop 'til they drop
down into ergonomic chairs
count goods & compute debt
touch edges of objects
unimaginably real & emptied
of desire already distracted by
the next act on Shopping TV
as long as they stay inside
there's nothing to hide

•

kids ask: what did you do in '68
at the gate behind the line
what did you do in the '50s
when Joe & Roy accused
did you answer did you fink
did you cut a deal
hesitate

take the 5th
bop back to Berlin
on cigarsmoke carpet
slip between silk Hollywood
butt-up take it pay your dues
sing them red blues forever
mea culprit I'm confessin'
that I love you

•

once I was a millionaire
brother can you spare a market share
some folks throw away pennies
others toss heaven into jars
everything adds upward
stars thick as bedbugs
tossed above our heads
gawk beyond clothesline stiff rags

•

From a Book of Revolutions
"men make their own history
but they do not make it just as they please
they don't make it under circumstances
chosen by themselves but under circumstances
directly encountered, given & transmitted
from the past. The tradition of all the dead
generations weighs like a nightmare
on the brain of the living" "war is
the highest form of struggle for
resolving contradictions" "thus
the rape of the Algerian woman
in the dream of European men
is always preceded
by a rending of the veil"

"stay awhile in the street
look at the passers-by
& remind yourself
the last word has not yet been said"

•

events now mostly memorials
wakes for gone ones passed over
& out to where
what rally in the sky
what workers' paradise
in a rented hall w/ a small band of old farts
w/ broken hearts going nowhere

•

broken bread crumbs in metal plate gutter
fingertips push into dry mouths
the start of prole cornucopia utopia
rolls down leather Ford beltways
watched by wage slaves
reading Gramsci

nobody needs the cars they want
or want the cars they need
stuck inside iron rationale estrangers go nowhere
on captive freeways held hostage to
construction crews

needs bleed trash
garbage age monumental pyramids
of stuff mulch stink rot deteriorate
into earth unable to digest it all
desire's crap devours horizon line

wounds whatever eats it sends toxins
through lifelines to death ends

left or right it's all over
red or black it's almost done
green or yellow what follows
can't be followed
everything remains
w/ no being to curse it

•

"god becomes man
infinity objectified in finitude
a finite spirit which remembers its infinity"
Hegel's bagel
Lenin's out by '23
sees Marxism as revolutionary
class praxis concerned (above all)
w/ conquest of power
capitalism's international
imperialism socialist
realism reification
hegemony & all of it
needs money for hives
to make honey class
conflict consciousness
bourgeois culture
desire for freedom
yen for happy
zen of exchange
trade fetish for fetish
regret nothing not even
bullet holes in pale skulls

•

forget revolt
regret what's yet to crash
give up history
maintain sinew
become a virus
try us & we renew

       ●

we're talking shirtsleeves
rolled up around arms whose hands
hold out cups for coin
disunion of unions what's left
but to organize begging

       ●

fall back into vodka tonic streams
sourdough pillow through towns
everyone cheers your triumph throws
brie-lathered pumpernickel morsels
wrapped in geranium blossoms mouthward
tossed rings of roses halo your hammer
chambray warrior floats downstream to
Big Rock Candy surrounded
by sincere banjo & guitar cacophony
as the river changes flavors

•

ginks & finks & company goons
shoot down the moon w/ buckshot
buttwards skid into halfassed graves
chowtime for rodents, rot rooters & wiggly worms
confirm jerky sinews succulent jaw munch
stooge scabs for Boss Scrooge nab lads
before they're out the door & plow them
pronto into dark bituminous Dante
quick buck & black lung long suck on
oxygen tank wheeled to bus stop to get to
Workman's Comp won't let you smoke
let you die while you wait for anybody
to cut a check or somebody to gurney you into ER
where deep down no one knows no real deal &
kids in white recoil behind the same old veil
there between you & the good life

•

fucking railroad brought it all down
robber barons Pinkertons corporations
standard issue lumpen desire
hack difference into mask code
appearance protocols

something manufactured
one size fits all

in a hurry to get away with it
in a hurry to blur particulars
in a hurry to devour
in a hurry to get over to
the other side a free ride
gold you can't imagine
but have to hold or have
some slug saronged in weightlifter belt
heft your load to the scale

in a hurry to get out of town before they catch on
in a hurry to lube wagon wheels & steal the map
peel away manners to worms behind mask
moving fast because nothing lasts

Tech

tech stipples chips out of metals
tech kicks steel pointed toe into throats
tech wrecks
tech builds
tech takes our breath away
tech talks for us anyway
tech walks away
tech stays out of eye range
tech stays neutral unless
tech bombs maps
tech makes bread
hand over fist
electronically wired
to feed itself while
flesh starves open handed
open ended pleas
even their pennies
tight in rolls
rolled to Bank
add up

tech talks light off the page
tech write rites off stage
tech's asana sits ergonomic
in plush back comfy chairs
to scan & scroll
to 80's rock 'n' roll
tech sees everywhere nowhere
at once & twice fractaled thrice
sliced Hermes wormy virus
through po mo's mainframe

tech talks spirit
but is material
virtual & other wise
techné the making
made thing man

golem ghettos
where no one goes
who wants to remain

techie the mechanic unwrecks the panic
of a higherpaid dreamer
in silicon hive of virtual jive
everyone staying alive in
puritan abundance

tech wrecks horizons
stacks waste in vast heaps
abandons once bright forms
in landfill darkness leeching
chemic blood of broken metals
into veins of homeless nomads
burn brains w/ fortified wine
whose bottlecaps kill

tech guts uncoiled spill into
battery acid pools haired w/
ancient wires rubber rot covers
reveal concealed copper threads
teeth chew on to eat
what moves in tech dump universe

tech stump hunk of gutless PC
on the sidewalk some kid will cop
home & pretend to be on line

tech talk & tech hard sell softens
dreamer loins w/ rotogravure
stains & sure pains of poverty
cities linked w/ lights she taps out
each ridge of spine disc hardwired
in seizure receive information's
measured pleasure locust tap tap

tech tonics designer sodas
imploded quotas ginseng mainframe
live forever atomized pixel virtual
face in space revolving planet
news of the world universal RKO

tech knocks clocks down to time
torment nano fractured second
of calibrated salary
each gesture a statistic on another screen's bank
blanks down a scroll of credit
crunch debit knives enter thorax
with ax force opera blood volcano aneurysm
tech tales told in rave caves
bounce off gs of decibels
imbeciles bob head first
fist fast into mosh pits where
junkie suicides reside
carpeting other bodies

tech tales geek speak
Wall Street speaker
Gates adjust rates for
alienated alien labor
down in micro sweatshops
popping chips into the boards
soldering info into a nation
that knows it's all over

tech solidarity drives
what's left of body dives
willingly within Buddhist pillow
packers or Saturday afternoon quarter
backers gulp down quarter pounders
angora cheerlead promos for more
of the same never changing flipbook
of goods fucking into more goods

on a cross the wheel hamsters plan
choice according to scheduled cycles
slice up life pasted onto successions of
confetti of never filled needs
your spaghetti guts spring forth
unquenchable bloody empty body out

tech bod whir clomp break down cast iron door
guarding treasure maps & circuit boards
pressed metal matzoh in rows stacked against
the wall wailing as the rest of us flail & slip on
greased ballroom marble MTV floors
into new age slide w/ old bones

tech in your head behind your eyes
fingernails buried inside follicles
transmit binary shit witless duh duh
buy sell space holograms shake your
booties to acid rave extasis whatever

tech grip unites the broken orb
unties any other why bother
tech top tips the scales e-mails
seconds before they start parting
cursor eye blink scanning
panning for gold

tech osophy theo grid saps
Sophia's bean & her old man
craps out of the loop
stoops to rancor the copped
chip dipped into enough snuff
to charge the Super Chief to Mars

tech talk brains on the march
vorticist horizontal extremes
insistence of Cézanne planes

& plain talk walks out the back door
wanting a refund a rebate
some recompense for nonsense

tech Mex hexed at the border
disordered & bruised sings
cantina blues to INS kids
still in love w/ their new guns
perfumed in oil boils their blood
ready or not for damage & grief

tech brain pro egghead
ineffectual intellectual power
in knowledge verathane vertical
hermetic peeled reelers roll
lines of banal lopped into office pools
sliding away in tight intrigue skirts
& Lands End shirts & everybody
alert to dirt beneath carpets new shoes
touch gently along the cracked facade

tech nicked color slime blood
feeds need ticks & knee jerk
parasites & paradoxes on compatible
stereo oh no not fields of story
disremembered dissing dat what's
in your face unremitting unquitting
sit on it read rubberstamp news
re done dance sweep up shadows

tech nays nature truth evaporates
on tonguetip slips away furled
inside your ear spiral
winds deep into a displaced space
soul's said to reside there upon her throne's song
throttled into cacophony délire

tech taught thought
wired through pre-school kids
mouse rocket games
count up carnage
new age oldtime nation-state
means what it meant then too
duck & unplug & run like hell
out of serene mall cage logic

tech new tomtom blips cursor
under eyelid spasm twitch itch
for more hard drive power
below the belt rocket pockets
shoot off batteries bringing forth
Anwesen Smith & Wesson
click cock unload das Enthbergen
Candice Bergen micro optical
connects US w/ a pin drop
techné a mode of revelation
of hearing & seeing all that's fit
to mint & impress class cage

& race rage & sexual fury
into psyches of Nike denying
acrobats of revolt w/ pliers
& stun guns of fun knock off
balance No's grind down

Breaking Up

—You're breaking up
he says in cellphone at corner of
16th & Valencia where earlier
a leathery black man pushing shopping cart, cigarette
burning between snarl lips
tells me I'm stupid
—You're breaking up
breaking down
breaking in
breaking up
breaking out

Append cell
to sellers & buyers
in a celled world
gated cells
broken hearts
broken bonds
breaking down
brake down
break apart
break dance

Celled & sold
hooked on
hooked in
hooked

Walk down broke
boulevards
disembody
—Hey, I'm here
what's up
talking to no one
seen or heard

Street Sheet lady
tells me about her
menopause—I'm
only 43 & am hot
or cold all the time & jump salty
& bark & bite back

—You're breaking up
as BART tunnels out of range
I'm broke
broken
that's the breaks
breaker breaker
heartbreaker

Hegemony
hedges gate the break
up into bytes &
bits of digital hell
walked through as Heaven

Hey, fart face
give a guy a break
a hands up
no finger
you know which one
lingers in insult
humiliate the broke
go for broke
break it all down
into rudimentary
shrapnel & electrodes
nodes implanted
microwave brain
drain w/ claims of
unity & community
& designer dogs &

white flight jogging
to Valhollywood of
immortality
—You're breaking up
he says
you're atomizing in my ear's
cloudchamber
can't hear you
fragments
then silence

—Hello
hello
are you there?

Alien(s)

it was a mistake
spirit not stuff
was the directive

middle management archon
screwed it up botched creation

I am called thinking of the invisible
I am called unchangeable voice
aeons of aeons
I ams of I ams

meat's the error
meet the terror
of failure of gravity
the weight of
stuckness

irritate the pearl of spirit's abandonment
hear me softly
& learn from me harshly

this time's the dream's on me

take light but leave dark
to guide the maze twist
of unanswered questions

the journey down
bondage
exodus
ascent to the royal realm

it is not I
the sound
of my thinking

am called
invisible thought
as we move
together
& separate
down industrial streets

hidden in all
revealed in all
each reaching out
to an other
stranger in despair

foreigners
displaced people
DPs
unrecognized
tagged as alien

alone
all one
no other
of you
for you

●

beyond usual bounds
or boundaries
foreign
strange

we came to believe
by means of signs & wonders
& fabrications
& emanation of trace

Check out the tape & tell me what you think.

"The alien is that which stems from elsewhere
& does not belong to here"

strange unfamiliar incomprehensible

lonely unprotected

"in the name of the great first alien Life
from the worlds of light"

the stranger who does not know the ways of the foreign land wanders
    about lost
lonely, unprotected, uncomprehended

not known nor seen as knowable
the stranger's lot

estranged from one's own origin
place
real estate

"alienness as superiority & suffering"
remoteness the fate of involvement

●

"The alien is that which stems from elsewhere and does not belong
here. To those who do belong here it is thus the strange, the
unfamiliar and incomprehensible; but their world in its part is just as
incomprehensible to the alien that comes to dwell here, and like a
foreign land where it is far from home."

●

liminal like the newborn teenager
unexpected
complex presence of you & those
who imagine themselves into a fictive life of us

•

played hooky from school
we woke up at 1:40 afternoon
sleeping through
the unlived life

•

the alien is that which stems from elsewhere
& doesn't belong here

if it learns
it forgets

extrangerio
lost from core
origin's tangles

•

the alien stems from elsewhere & does not belong here

to those who belong here it is strange & unfamiliar incomprehensible

but their world
just as alien

the stranger is lonely & suffers uprootedness
uncomprehended
unknowing
in a situation
full of danger

anguish
homesickness
the stranger's lot

learn the ways too well
& forget one is a stranger
gets lost in a new way

succumb to the alien world's allure
is to be further estranged
from origin

•

she takes shazanda
I do melatonin
to sleep & dream
lost on awakening

her dreams are of houses
mine of cities

"I feel as if I were drugged"

•

collective we of multiples
came to this place
to melt into that pot
"I cried & worried all night I lays & groans
I used to weigh 200
now I'm down to skin & bones"

                    •

the soul slumbers in matter
silent in Lucite
ambergris
stopped

would that
a great voice
come daily to
awaken me
break the spell
halt the shuffle trance

                         •

"what liberates us is the knowledge of who we were, what we became;
where we were, where into we've been thrown; where to we speed,
wherefore we are redeemed; what birth is & rebirth"

                         •

grain's dark
even staring into light

            •

brought here
not wanting to be here
pushed onto lines

that rarely move or end
whatever I tell an official
is another language
misunderstood

beyond the paper & rubber stamps
nibbed ink scratch
on government parchment
blue lines
blotted in a hurry
blur surname
where were we
now that we're here?

●

they come from the sky
cross oceans
wherever they land
they do not belong

●

inside or outside
prison contains
unwingable flight
the locked door
is freedom for those
w/out it
but those w/in it
cry diamonds into
burnt-out leather smuggler pouches

●

nature did not destine us
for a base ignoble existence

if someone could look at the world from on high
& behold the wealth of beauty in it
he would know
what we were born for

walls & veils diversions
labyrinths & mazes
the path as challenge unfolds in faith

"the unconscious is a veritable infection
by the poison of darkness
they mixed my drink w/ cunning
& gave me a taste of meat
I forgot I was a king's son

through the heaviness of their nourishment
I sink into a deep slumber"

•

it's the slime
that keeps division divided

it's a sci-fi cliché
it's fucking X Files
lightless creep holes where
dim flashlights skid off
weird alien slick slather

snot rugs pulled out
prosthetic clots
slip over into new
bone smash
configure
go figure
the broken & perfect

alive or dead in sepia snaps retrieved out of
spored boxes of darkness

was in the was
& is in that same was-ness
where one is nowhere stuck in all of it

                    •

ground zero
where alphabet recircles itself
back to Aleph & its razors of imprint
whose wounds
slash veils while
spider like spit out
new webs to weave outcry
inactive & consumed

                •

re-member torn away
wings & thing
that danced
on illumined stages

            •

the stuff which unpuffs & blurts out intestines & the usual FX

the stuff which means nothing
but everything
the stuff which decays & is poetry
the goo the snot the rot

alive as we die
no myth but being
no being but myth

no no
die to be
to birth
to burst
forth

•

Aya's sure she's an ET
as well as a Pharaonic Egyptian goddess & multigenerational physician
of all kinds of medicine

all I remember is drowning
& breaking through

•

"otherness"
alias moniker
masked vapor
unknowable
"belonging to
another person
another place" something else
not knowable
a distraction from what is

a challenge
a threat
the obvious

●

life heat of all internal organs grinds down to soot

bone cold hexagram telegrams
dot dot common amnesia
aphasia dementia
can't remember
can't forget
what is it
who
me?

cape me
big brim hat me
mask me
ask me the meaning of life
& if I say strife
tire-shoe me
retire me
as long as you know
nothing rules
only unknowing
opens up the books
rescrambles the letters
chains them back to fetters
stutter to blank melody
dots chained to staffs
horizontal lines
ruled

●

each amazed wing feather
spread & fanned &
plucked for pens
whose bone nibs dip
deep into inkwells

•

Up against the wall
Caligari style
to slide away
duck spotlights
angry driven dogs
dissolve in dark cover

set apart from
what beholds
& holds all
together
in the vision
of blank
sight of
vapor ineffable
w/ affable spew
of metaphor's faith
in lingo to link
all together in one
pure mirrored wall

•

The opinions of people concerning prophecy are like their opinions
concerning the eternity of the world or its creation in time

yes yes
why wait when
time breaks down
fails to exist
in axes of remove
chop chop
your hand reaching out for
the promised land

Bibliography

Poetry

Poems. David Meltzer/Donald Schenker. Printed privately by Donald & Alice Schenker, San Francisco.

Ragas. San Francisco: Discovery Books, 1959.

The Clown. Larkspur: Semina, 1960.

Bazascope Mother. Los Angeles: Drekfesser Press, 1964.

The Process. Berkeley: Oyez, 1965.

Oyez! Berkeley: Oyez, 1967.

The Dark Continent. Berkeley: Oyez, 1967.

Journal of the Birth. Berkeley: Oyez, 1967.

From Eden Book. (Maya Quarto Four.) San Francisco: Cranium Press, 1969.

Round the Poem Box: Rustic and Domestic Home Movies for Stan and Jane Brakhage. Santa Barbara: Black Sparrow Press, 1969.

Yesod. London: Trigram Press, 1969.

Luna. Los Angeles: Black Sparrow Press, 1970.

Greenspeech. Goleta, California: Christopher Books, 1970.

Isla Vista Notes: Fragmentary Apocalyptic Didactic Contradictions. Santa Barbara: Christopher Books, 1970.

Knots. Bolinas, California: Tree Books, 1971.

Tens: Selected Poems. Edited by Kenneth Rexroth. New York: McGraw-Hill, 1973.

Hero/Lil. Santa Barbara: Black Sparrow Press, 1973.

Bark, A Polemic. Santa Barbara: Yes! Capra Press, 1973.

The Eyes, The Blood. San Francisco: Mudra, 1973.

French Broom. Berkeley: Oyez, 1973.

Blue Rags. Berkeley: 1974.

Harps. Berkeley: Oyez, 1975.

Boléro. Berkeley: Oyez, 1976.

Six. Santa Barbara: Black Sparrow Press, 1976.

Abra. Illustrated by John Brandi. Berkeley: Hipparchia, 1976.

The Art/The Veil. Milwaukee: Membrane Press, 1981.

The Name: Selected Poetry 1973–1983. Santa Barbara: Black Sparrow Press, 1984.

Arrows: Selected Poetry 1957–1992. Santa Rosa: Black Sparrow Press, 1994.

No Eyes: Lester Young. Santa Rosa: Black Sparrow Press, 2000.
Beat Thing. Albuquerque: La Alameda Press, 2004.

Fiction

How Many Blocks in the Pile? Hollywood: Essex House, 1968.
The Agent. Hollywood: Essex House, 1968.
The Agency. Hollywood: Essex House, 1968.
Orf. Hollywood: Essex House, 1968.
Lovely: The Brain-Plant, Book 1. Hollywood: Essex House, 1969.
Healer: The Brain-Plant, Book 2. Hollywood: Essex House, 1969.
Out: The Brain-Plant, Book 3. Hollywood: Essex House, 1969.
Glue Factory: The Brain-Plant, Book 4. Hollywood: Essex House, 1969.
Star. Hollywood: Brandon House, 1970.
Tendre Reseau. French translation of *The Agency* by Maxim Jakubowski.
    Paris: Editions Champ Libre, 1977.
Two-Way Mirror: A Poetry Notebook. Berkeley: Oyez, 1977.
The Agency Trilogy. New York: Masquerade Books, 1994.
Under. New York: Rhinoceros Books, 1995.

Editor

Meltzer, David [editor]. *The San Francisco Poets*. New York: Ballantine
    Books, 1971.
———. *Golden Gate: Interviews with Five San Francisco Poets*. Berkeley:
    Wingbow Press, 1976.
———. *The Secret Garden: An Anthology in the Kabbalah*. New York:
    Seabury Press, 1976.
———. *Birth: An Anthology of Ancient Texts, Songs, Prayers, and Stories*.
    San Francisco: North Point Press, 1981.
———. *Death: An Anthology of Texts, Songs, Charms, Prayers, and Tales*.
    San Francisco: North Point Press, 1984.
———. *Reading Jazz*. San Francisco: Mercury House, 1993.
———. *Writing Jazz*. San Francisco: Mercury House, 1999.
———. *San Francisco Beat: Talking with the Poets*. San Francisco: City
    Lights Books, 2001.

Essays

We All Have Something to Say to Each Other: Being an Essay Entitled Kenneth Patchen and Four Poems. San Francisco: Auerhahn Press, 1962.

Recordings

Serpent Power. Vanguard Records, 1968. Reissued on CD in 1996.

Poet Song. Vanguard Records, 1969.

Green Morning. Capitol Records, 1970, unreleased, issued on vinyl from a Swiss company in 1999; CD 2002.

Serpent Power/Poet Song. Italy, 2000.

David Meltzer Reads Poetry with Jazz, 1959. Sierra Records, 2005. Los Angeles.

Other

Naoya, Shiga. *Morning Glories.* Translated by David Meltzer and Allen Say. Berkeley: Oyez, 1976.

About the Author

Born in Rochester at the finale of the Great Depression in 1937 of bohemian parents (she a harpist, he a cellist), immigrated to Brooklyn in 1940 where I was educated fully in the red-wing zone of immigrants, radicals, orthodoxies, & obsessive baseball statistics essential to overall nourishment in that vibrant matrix. Became a poet when I was 11 & my first poem was about the NYC subway system. (Read all the down & dirty details in *Two-Way Mirror: A Poetry Notebook*, Oyez, 1977.) Was also a child performer on radio & early TV—a regular irregular on the *Horn & Hardart Children's Hour*. Graduated from nothing, not even grade school. Was I.Q. over-endowed & put into accelerated public school programs that weren't acknowledged when my family migrated to Rockville Centre. Was accepted into the University of Chicago's program for obnoxiously smart preteens, but my parents didn't want me to go. Afraid of tommy *guns*. I became, thus, a chain-smoking paperback-reading mutant hardly ever appearing in class. No grade school certificate, no junior high school artifact, nada nada. By the time I came to Los Angeles w/ my father (the family broke apart), I had a steamer trunk full of Joyce, James T. Farrell, John Dos Passos, Carl Sandburg, Faulkner, Céline, Patchen, Anaïs Nin, Henry Miller, & others of that time & beyond that time too numerous to mention. Little clothing but mucho books & immense tonnage of typing stuffing the steamer.

Left Brooklyn with my father for "the Coast," Los Angeles, in 1954. Culture shock. Continued my sabbatical from high school & worked at an open-air newsstand on Western Avenue & Hollywood Boulevard encountering many lofty & sleazoid Hollywood types. Went back to school when I was almost 18—Fairfax High in the heart of left-wing Jewish haimish hoedowns. Barely a sophomore according to the public school hierarchy. Mr. Quick, my English teacher & the first vegetarian I ever met, brought his lunch to school, usually home-curdled yogurt, organic fruit, wheat germ. He asked me to share it w/ him one afternoon. "Look, Meltzer, you're too long in the tooth to be here & you & I know you can write & think. Take an equivalency test at L.A. City College & see if it challenges your abilities." Which I did. The first semester I attended during the day & worked across the street at the Pepper Tree Gardens, a hamburger joint run by two in & out of work actors, where one of them initiated me into a deep Duke Ellington groove. Started hanging out w/ jazz musicians rehearsing on campus. More important, was a full-time student in the school of Wallace Berman, Robert Alexander, Ed Keinholz, John Altoon, George Herms, Charles Britten, Artie Richer, John Kelley Reed, artists who by some rare convergence constituted an emergent force in postwar art. L.A. at that time was not that much of a word town as it was a visual arts scene. Found the level of City College teaching & student brain power boring, decided to try night courses figuring adults would be more strongly motivated & might jolt the engine. No way; was on my own way under the tutelage of working artists & jazz musicians & young actors, ex–child stars, eccentrics & tricksters.

Migrated to San Francisco in 1957; immediately fell into the North Beach cultural revolutions which became too quickly co-opted by media & the tendency to one-dimensionalize dissidence into defanged cuddly types like Maynard G. Krebs. Met Tina who became my wife, lover, partner, collaborator for almost 37 years. We began performing together during the '60s folk revival & graduated into a folk-rock band w/ psychedelic overtones. Three CDs of that moment currently available via the Net.

Author of a decalogue of agit-smut novels in the late '60s which vortexed into the abyss of banishment similar to the 99¢ store graveyard—which endlessly fascinate & haunt this geezer—the pathos of abundance. *The Agency Trilogy* was reissued in a one-volume edition by R. Kasak Books in the late '90s.

Most recent book of poetry is *Beat Thing* (La Alameda Press, 2004), and am the editor and interviewer for *San Francisco Beat: Talking with the Poets* (City Lights, 2001). Teach in the graduate Poetics program at New College of California, as well as in its outstanding undergraduate Humanities program. With Steve Dickison, co-edit *Shuffle Boil,* a one-of-a-kind magazine devoted to music in all its appearances & disappearances. Too much more, too little time.

Penguin Poets

TED BERRIGAN
The Sonnets

PHILIP BOOTH
*Lifelines: Selected Poems
1950–1999*

JIM CARROLL
*Fear of Dreaming:
The Selected Poems
Living at the Movies
Void of Course*

BARBARA CULLY
Desire Reclining

ALISON HAWTHORNE
DEMING
Genius Loci

CARL DENNIS
*New and Selected Poems
1974–2004
Practical Gods
Ranking the Wishes*

DIANE DI PRIMA
Loba

STUART DISCHELL
Dig Safe

STEPHEN DOBYNS
*Mystery, So Long
Pallbearers Envying the One
Who Rides
The Porcupine's Kisses
Velocities: New and
Selected Poems:
1966–1992*

ROGER FANNING
Homesick

AMY GERSTLER
*Crown of Weeds
Ghost Girl
Medicine
Nerve Storm*

EUGENE GLORIA
*Drivers at the Short-Time
Motel*

DEBORA GREGER
*Desert Fathers, Uranium
Daughters
God
Western Art*

TERRANCE HAYES
Hip Logic

ROBERT HUNTER
Sentinel and Other Poems

BARBARA JORDAN
Trace Elements

MARY KARR
Viper Rum

WILLIAM KECKLER
Sanskrit of the Body

JACK KEROUAC
*Book of Blues
Book of Haikus*

JOANNE KYGER
As Ever: Selected Poems

ANN LAUTERBACH
*Hum
If in Time: Selected Poems,
1975–2000
On a Stair*

CORINNE LEE
PYX

PHYLLIS LEVIN
Mercury

WILLIAM LOGAN
*Macbeth in Venice
Night Battle
Vain Empires
The Whispering Gallery*

MICHAEL MCCLURE
*Huge Dreams: San
Francisco and Beat
Poems*

DAVID MELTZER
*David's Copy: The Selected
Poems of David Meltzer*

CAROL MUSKE
*An Octave Above Thunder
Red Trousseau*

ALICE NOTLEY
*The Descent of Alette
Disobedience
Mysteries of Small Houses*

LAWRENCE RAAB
*The Probable World
Visible Signs: New and
Selected Poems*

PATTIANN ROGERS
Generations

LEE ANN RORIPAUGH
Beyond Heart Mountain

STEPHANIE STRICKLAND
*V: WaveSon.nets/Losing
L'una*

ANNE WALDMAN
*Kill or Cure
Marriage: A Sentence
Structure of the World
Compared to a Bubble*

JAMES WELCH
Riding the Earthboy 40

PHILIP WHALEN
Overtime: Selected Poems

SUSAN WOOD
Asunder

ROBERT WRIGLEY
*Lives of the Animals
Reign of Snakes*

MARK YAKICH
*Unrelated Individuals
Forming a Group Waiting
to Cross*

JOHN YAU
Borrowed Love Poems